6-4-74

Power to the Public Worker

RICHARD N. BILLINGS
JOHN GREENYA

POWER
TO THE
PUBLIC
WORKER

Robert B. Luce, Inc.   Washington-New York

1804058

Contents

Introduction

In the spring of 1966 I was assigned by *Life Magazine* to report on the state of the American labor movement. It was the sort of job that writers try to avoid, not unlike being told to go do a story on the Yukon Territory, one that requires months of rambling about trying to fix a focus on the subject, striving for journalistic judgments that won't appear to be prejudices.

It was a time when labor was ripe for criticism. Senate hearings on corruption and racket influences were recent enough to be easily remembered, and Jimmy Hoffa was headed for the federal penitentiary. Wage demands were often exceeding the guidelines President Johnson insisted were necessary to flag down inflation, and in the summer an outbreak of strike fever served to arouse a temper of antagonism in the American public.

The main theme of the *Life* article, however, dealt with neither corruption nor economics, for it was a none too startling discovery that the human qualities of labor's leadership were the subject of most significance. Tenacious, old, out of touch with their members and out of step with each other were the descriptive words and phrases used to describe the hierarchy of the AFL–CIO.

The merged federation, a little over ten years in existence, was the arena of a bitter feud between George Meany, then 72, who though remote and conservative ruled with an iron fist, and Walter Reuther, whose inability to be an effective voice from within would cause him shortly before his death to lead his United Auto Workers out of the AFL–CIO.

It was only natural to seek a leader who would be the exception that proved the rule. The answer was Jerry Wurf, described in a headline when the story appeared as a "young militant out to unionize city and country employees." He turned out to be much more than an exception.

The time was right for Wurf. It had been just two years since he had taken over the American Federation of State, County and Municipal Employees, following a protracted campaign against the presidency of Arnold Zander, the union's founder, but they had been watershed years. He was (and is) young and dynamic, especially in contrast to the majority of international union presidents, but, most important, Wurf was at the vanguard of a revolution in American labor.

On a swing through Ohio and Michigan in June Wurf spread the message forcefully and with passion to his members—zookeepers, hospital attendants, sanitation men and custodians. The time for us is now, he would say, as it was for the industrial unions in the thirties. And in Lansing, after an all-night bargaining session with the mayor, he showed his muscle by leading an illegal strike.

To many who must deal with him—especially the mayors and other officials across the table—Wurf can be obstinate, obnoxious and exasperating. In his glib manner of speaking he draws effectively from the resources of his alert mind, and his sentences, spoken with an accent that is all Brooklyn, are punctuated with four-letter words, not so much an assortment but a repetition of the single, most common adjective that is still offensive in polite society. (His ability to communicate verbally is so effective, in fact, that much of this story is told in Wurf's own colorful, reflective words.)

Wurf deserves credit for sensing it was time for public employee unionism to achieve collective bargaining and other

8

advantages enjoyed by trade and industrial unions and for grabbing the initiative and leading the fight against Zander. But there were numerous other young "red-hots" in high positions at AFSCME during the fifties, and it is significant that Wurf emerged as their leader.

John Greenya and I put forth extensive effort in the course of writing this book to determine the decisive differences between the Zander administration and the forces of rebellion that were eventually successful in Denver in 1964. Many factors were contributory, but none fully answered the question. It was partly a matter of age—new and restless leaders versus old and traditional incumbents, the ins against the outs. The major philosophical disagreement was, of course, the extent to which a public employee union should fight for improved wages, hours and working conditions and ultimately the right to strike against the state. Finally, there was the tendency to explain it as an urban versus rural, big versus little jurisdiction, though the case falls apart on close inspection.

In the end we concluded it all came down to a Wurf-Zander confrontation, partly personal, partly philosophical but, more importantly, the product of geographic orientation and a record of accomplishment.

While Arnold Zander was a product of Wisconsin progressivism, the social experiment and one of the very first civil service systems, Jerry Wurf was slugging his way up from picket lines in Brooklyn and adhering to the faith of Fabian socialism, although his political attitudes were to soften in later years. Wurf's early admiration for Zander was to expire over basic differences that were more practical than philosophic, however. His record of stewardship in New York best explains their falling out as well as the inevitability of Wurf's being chosen to lead the rebellion.

For eight years before being elected international president, Wurf ran District Council 37 in New York, first as an international representative and later as its director. There is much to support his contention today that D.C. 37 was an incubator for ideas and action that were to be translated into progress for the whole union:

- In 1957, after a long fight in Congress resulted in federal enabling legislation, AFSCME led the fight in New York to extend full social security coverage to all public employees.
- On July 1, 1959 District Council 37 signed its first collective bargaining agreement covering 40 categories of workers in parks and museums and providing raises. For the first time the union bargained for new job titles that could upgrade thousands of workers.
- On May 18, 1961, following a six-week strike, workers at the Bronx Zoo and Coney Island Aquarium signed their first contract providing for a complete grievance procedure, arbitration for all challenged discharges and a ten percent pay raise.
- In December 1962 a new contract was signed for motor vehicle operators of AFSCME Local 983, providing for an unprecedented, city financed, union administered welfare fund which by now contains millions of dollars.

Despite his rasping manner, Wurf's personality is engaging, his brilliant, outspoken attitudes stimulating, and he has been able to enlist absolute loyalty from associates, though in the ever competitive world of trade unionism it is sometimes begrudging. Wurf is also admired outside the immediate circle, and it is on a few close trade union associates, not all his subordinates, that he has relied for support and advice. Three men in particular are most often mentioned by Wurf.

One is Paul Hall, president of the Seafarers International Union, a modern and public-spirited labor leader but in many ways a character opposite of Wurf. A burly Alabamian, Hall is said to have told a mutual friend in the forties that damned if he wanted to meet another of his socialist cronies, but he and Wurf did meet and became close friends. Hall's seamen backed up Wurf on the barricades during those early AFSCME strikes in New York, and their alliance continues to this day, despite the fact that Hall is one of labor's few supporters of President Nixon, while Wurf is its most dedicated Nixon hater.

Another is the late Eric Polisar, a Cornell economics professor who at the time of his untimely death in 1969 was a close confidant and intellectual advisor of Wurf. Polisar, a leftist in the thirties and later an organizer for the amalgamated clothing workers in the south, was a man of strong principles (though quite irreverent) with a sound, analytical mind. He was not afraid to tell Wurf he was wrong, which he often did, especially when he thought Wurf was moving in a position of accommodation with the labor movement establishment.

The third is Victor H. Gotbaum, one of the early fighters for reform of the union and today executive director of AFSCME's District Council 37, the New York City employees' union. Gotbaum is one of the most influential figures in the union, sophisticated and highly articulate. He is also New York bred and from the same generation as Wurf, but he tends to be softer spoken, more reflective, although at times less compromising.

Wurf's accommodation is hardly noticeable, though he can be pragmatic, and his admiration for Meany is surprising considering their many differences. What guides Wurf more than anything is a strong sense of morality and decency, the two principles to which he is most loyal. He can laugh playfully about such sins as drinking, smoking and woman chasing—though he is personally abstemious—but the morality he cares about has to do with a fair shake for the worker, keeping promises and living up to standards he believes in. His ability to articulate and follow this code has been a major reason for his success.

11

Another reason is the fourth person to whom he has turned for advice, the former AFSCME staff member who became his wife in 1960. Mildred Wurf has her own thoughts about the success of the union and its future, and in her quiet, thoughtful way she can be just as articulate as her husband.

Busily engaged in activities not involved with her husband's union, including volunteer work and raising their two young children, Mildred does, however, attend the biennial AFSCME conventions, and when she goes to Honolulu in the spring of this year, it will be her ninth in a row. These conventions symbolize for her the heterogeneous quality of the union that is its hallmark. "A very substantial mix of people is represented—Trotskyites, militant blacks, New York liberals, back country folk and especially middle Americans—and they come together to make decisions that will affect their entire lives. That to me is the essence of democracy."

For Mildred the greatest significance of the union lies in two areas, one political, the other social. The political action education program—consisting of field workshops on voter registration, fund raising, etc.—is, she feels, the most effective in the labor movement, especially so since the heterogeneous nature of the union spreads its results across a broad slice of American life. And in the social field the union is special, she believes, because it is deeply involved in human services and institutions—prisons, hospitals, schools—at a time when these institutions are under attack for not responding to change. "The future of this union," she is convinced, "is the ability to be a bridge between social needs and the people who respond to them."

Richard N. Billings

January 1974

12

1.   From Civil Service Origins
to AFL Accreditation

*At meetings of the AFL-CIO executive council, says
one insider, the vote usually ranges from 25 to 1 to
34 to 1, depending on how many other union chiefs
are present to vote down Jerry Wurf.*

TIME, May 21, 1973

Just as Jerry Wurf represents the growth and strength of
the American Federation of State, County and Municipal
Employees during the past decade, the man who symbolized
its early growth was Arnold Zander, its only president until
1964.

George Meany never really favored the quiet, scholarly
Arnold Zander, original president of AFSCME, who once described himself as "Bill Green's boy." When Meany succeeded Green as AFL–CIO president, "I was out," Zander says.

Despite their many differences Meany is much closer to
the trade unionism of Jerry Wurf than to the philosophy of
Zander. Meany may not always appreciate the blunt, often
angry outbursts of Wurf, but one concludes that the old man,
looking down the council table at the AFSCME president of ten
years standing, feels more comfortable with him than he ever
would have with Zander.

13

In 1930 Zander was senior personnel examiner for the state of Wisconsin, which had the most effective civil service system in the nation. (In 1905 Wisconsin became the second state to enact a civil service law.) The director of the state Civil Service system was Col. A.E. Garey. Garey was a founder of the union and for many years would continue to play an important behind the scenes role in its development. Garey, Zander's superior, was a man whose belief in civil service legislation both influenced and complemented Zander's own populist-socialist philosophy.

With Progressive Phillip LaFollette in the governor's office in 1932 the atmosphere was ideal for organizing public employees. In fact, when Garey and the head of the Wisconsin State Federation of Labor, Frederick Ohl, went to seek the support of the governor in the spring of 1932, LaFollette expressed surprise they hadn't come to him earlier.

In the modern definition of trade unionism it was a curious way to establish a union, because not only the governor but Garey and Zander as well were aligned with state management; they were the bosses with whom union leadership would normally negotiate. But they were faced with a serious problem: their civil service was in danger of political assault, so they turned to union organization to protect the system.

Unlike some state and local bureaucrats Garey and Zander did not oppose the labor movement. They were progressive liberals who promptly accepted LaFollette's backing in establishing a union of Wisconsin state employees at a time when such a state affiliation was a rarity.

In May 1932 the Wisconsin State Administrative, Clerical Fiscal and Technical Employees Association was created (though its name was soon changed to the Wisconsin State Administrative Employees Association and then again to the Wisconsin State Employees Association).

Arnold Zander was elected financial secretary. He expected that the power of a young organization like the WSEA

14

The Boston police strike of 1919 which has come to symbolize militant unionism among public employees

was held by the man who controlled the purse strings, and he was able to use the position to expand the organization beyond the borders of Wisconsin. Although there were little over 50 members in 1932, the WSEA was formed at a propitious time. Fewer and fewer jobs were to be had, and the person with a protected job was in an enviable spot. Under Garey's direction the Wisconsin civil service system had progressed to the point where all state employees, save teachers and a few administrators, held their jobs by virtue of competitive examinations. Jobs and promotions were based on merit and service. But civil service was a system effective only so long as the civil service act was not repealed. An organization such as WSEA was needed to protect the system.

The depression by 1932 had caused unemployment for hundreds of thousands of Wisconsin workers whose jobs were not protected by the civil service system. Protest marches on city hall were commonplace, and on election day the Democrats were able to capture the state.

When Franklin D. Roosevelt was swept into the White House, he carried with him Albert G. Schmederman, the first Democratic governor of Wisconsin in 40 years. Not surprisingly, the new administration coveted the many state jobs that were no longer, as in most states, fair game for the spoils system. It didn't take long for the attack on civil service to get underway in Madison.

On January 17, 1933 a Democratic senator introduced a bill containing two clauses that would effectively scuttle the civil service system. The WSEA leadership was startled, for it had been prepared for less sweeping measures. It turned to the American Federation of Labor for help.

AFL President William Green responded to a plea from Zander by sending Paul Smith, a professional union organizer, to advise the WSEA on strategy. Smith had come to Wisconsin the previous year to apprise Zander and Garey of AFL charter requirements; now he was back to help the young union survive.

16

Zander and Garey, in turn, were able to give Smith a better understanding of the type of public worker the union could attract, for the most part white-collar engineers, auditors and civil service examiners. And they were able to work with Smith in getting their new membership organized. Meetings were held—there were even marches and demonstrations—as the public employees of Wisconsin had their first experience with true union activity and the kind of collective effectiveness that would enable them to stand up to the state government.

The Democrats were nearly able to destroy one of the few effective civil service structures in the country in favor of the old game of political payoff. But organized lobbying by the WSEA leadership defeated the bill, and the union made a name for itself.

By June 1933 its membership consisted of 700 of the 1,700 eligible public employees. This rather outstanding accomplishment was noticed in other states, and Zander was able to spread the new gospel of public worker organization around the country.

WSEA's charter made it a federal local of the AFL for Wisconsin employees, but as Zander soon realized, there was little future in that arrangement. The membership potential was too small, the budget too limited. But he did perceive the future of a national union of public employees.

Zander began talking up the idea of a national union of state, county and municipal employees, and with AFL encouragement (three months salary), he began to travel outside Wisconsin to promote his notion. A potential nucleus existed. WSEA was one of just a few federal locals affiliated with the AFL, but there were other non-affiliated unions. In New York, for example, 12,000 public workers were organized.

Although there were some encouraging signs that the AFL would grant the WSEA a separate charter as a national union of state, county and city employees, they were premature and misleading. In October 1934 the AFL took action that threat-

17

ened to destroy Zander's dream. Its executive council passed a resolution to affiliate the WSEA and the American Federation of Government Employees, with AFGE, a federal workers' union, as the dominant partner. Earlier in the year AFGE had amended its own constitution to allow it to organize state, county and municipal employees.

Zander had assumed that his union would grow in much the same fashion as AFGE and with its support, so the news that AFGE, with AFL sanction, intended to swallow him up came as a severe shock. He went to the AFL convention in May 1935 to try to convince Green and the executive council to reverse their decision and grant his union a separate charter for local and state employees.

He did manage to meet with Green, but unfortunately for Zander the AFL had more serious concerns. There was a schism in the ranks of the AFL that ultimately led to the formation of the Congress of Industrial Organizations. The only compromise Zander was able to achieve was a deal with AFGE President E. Claude Babcock. Babcock agreed that Zander's national union, by then called the American Federation of State, County and Municipal Employees, would be able to affiliate with the AFL through AFGE. AFSCME therefore became a department of AFGE. But even though AFSCME members would pay dues to AFGE, Zander was assured that his organization would be autonomous and coequal with that of the federal employees.

Zander was disappointed with the arrangement and wasn't ready to desert his fight for independence. Moreover, there were complaints from his members over the condescending treatment and paternalistic attitudes of AFGE leadership.

Zander wrote to Frank Morrison, secretary of the AFL, on September 13, 1935:

> I know beyond any question of doubt that right now a national union with jurisdiction over state, county, and city employees, following the lines of the American Federation of Government Employ-

ees, could be launched with remarkable success, and should be started for many reasons which I know you and President Green and the executive council would appreciate . . . I know something about government and public employees. I can see just across the horizon the development of a nation-wide affiliation of civil service employee associations. This is coming. The question before us is not whether a national organization is to be formed, but whether or not this national is to be affiliated with the organized labor movement.

The original setback had occurred because Zander wasn't the only one who could see a national union of public employees "just across the horizon." Now that the AFL and AFGE had moved to change the structure of the union from that Zander and his group had first visualized, he and his following realized they might well lose the support of some of their locals if the situation were not quickly resolved. Throughout the summer and fall following the May convention they continued the plans made before May for a constitutional convention for state and local employees in Chicago in December 1935.

Zander was in a difficult position: some of his members would have been satisfied with the arrangement worked out in Atlantic City, but others were excited about the original idea of a separate, totally autonomous union of nonfederal public employees.

As his own sentiments were clearly with the latter group, Zander pressed on with plans for AFSCME's first convention, against the advice of AFL President Green.

Green, in a letter dated November 20, 1935, urged Zander to call a later convention and concluded, ". . . I feel confident the agreement will prove to be acceptable to the executive council and that it will be given its official endorsement."

Zander replied five days later:

... If it were your intention to take up with the executive council the question of jurisdictional assignment and if we had some hope of securing our own charter, we could more gracefully suffer the delay you suggest. If, on the other hand, the question is merely one of endorsement of an arrangement within an international union regarding a matter referred to you by the executive council, it seems to me we should not postpone taking a step which is so urgent.

Convention arrangements have been completed. We are to meet at ten o'clock on the morning of December 9 at the Hotel Morrison in Chicago. The federal locals affected have been notified. During the last week I have met with approximately a dozen of them. They have chosen delegates. Delegates have arranged time off, in some cases at considerable inconvenience. The date December 9 was suggested by President Babcock in a telegram sent to us early this month. It has been my hope that you would find it possible to meet with us, and I have suggested this possibility in my efforts to arouse the federal locals.

Zander also employed some political persuasion with Green, implying in the letter that he might be able to strike a better deal with John L. Lewis' CIO.

The December convention went on as scheduled. Green was absent, but it had been agreed that AFGE officials would come even though it was entirely Zander's show.

Babcock arrived in Chicago specifically for the meeting, but he never reached the convention hall. Instead the AFGE president went to jail. Zander, a devout Christian Scientist and teetotaler, recounted the incident almost 40 years later. "Babcock arrived the night before the convention and was having a drink with some friends in a bar. After a few drinks an argument began, which Babcock ended by getting up and throwing a bottle through the mirror behind the bar. It seems that such conduct was frowned upon, and he found himself in jail."

The AFSCME membership showed strong sentiment for independence. The convention adopted a constitution modeled on that of AFGE, but any affinity of interest ended there. The movement begun by the formation of WSEA three years before reached a climactic point when the convention elected Arnold Zander president and Roy E. Kubista, another Wisconsinite, secretary-treasurer. Kubista, who joined the union right out of college, has spent his entire career with AFSCME as a state council director and international staff official.

The new organization, though still technically a department of AFGE, scheduled its first annual convention for September 1936. Zander, Kubista and their followers—even Col. Garey stepped from behind the scenes to join the campaign— were all going out for separation and total autonomy.

In a letter to Green on January 25, 1936 Garey warned, "If you make an effort to organize these people with the federal employees, Zander will be out in the cold talking to himself about the value of American Federation of Labor affiliation, but he won't have a following. You will have a loyal lieutenant without a company. . ."

When the AFL executive council met in January 1936, Green announced that the agreement between AFSCME and AFGE, worked out after the 1935 convention in Atlantic City, was falling apart. He read a request from Zander for a separate charter. The council voted to defer action but asked President Green to try to resolve the difficulty.

Green was able to get the two unions to agree to maintain a status quo until the annual AFGE convention in Detroit the coming fall.

The situation changed favorably for Zander when Babcock found himself in trouble with his own membership. Apparently they didn't take to the idea of their president

21

being jailed for barroom scrapes and other escapades, and a recall proceeding had been started. On June 15 he was suspended with pay pending a determination of his case. (Some AFGE members approached Zander and asked if he would be interested in the presidency of their union, but Zander, close to realizing his dream of a separate union of state and municipal employees, declined.)

During this period correspondence between Zander and Babcock had been sharp and occasionally angry. Professionally the two men were natural rivals, and their personality differences did not ease the rivalry. But with the AFGE president powerless for the moment, the relationship between AFSCME and AFGE improved.

Zander asked AFGE's acting president, Bernice Heffner, for permission to address AFGE's executive council just before the AFGE convention in September, but then decided to submit a written statement instead.

Zander listed the reasons why he felt the two unions had to be separate. He maintained that no authorities in "political science, public administration, or organized labor" could be cited to support joining state, county and municipal employees with federal employees. It was organizationally unsound because the federal employees had to deal with Congress and nonfederal public workers with whatever state or local government employed them.

> Imagine us appearing before the executive council of the AFL and winning a limited. . . jurisdiction over you. . . . Imagine us getting that right without consulting you or giving you the right to be heard. Imagine us calling ourselves your parent body and exacting tribute from you. . . offering you nothing in return. Imagine us assuming an attitude of superiority toward you. Imagine the circumstances reversed.

Zander's statement told the AFGE council what many of

22

them already knew, and a changed attitude toward AFSCME was demonstrated by actions taken at the convention. Although it was voted once again to allow membership of state, county and municipal employees, the AFGE executive council was authorized by the convention to relinquish its jurisdiction over AFSCME if that were to be the recommendation of the AFL executive council.

In late September 1936 AFSCME's convention opened with an address by George Googe, representative of AFL President Green, who revealed the action of the AFGE convention. And on the final day Charles Stengle, president-elect of AFGE, read a letter signed by a committee of the AFGE executive council recommending a separate AFL charter for AFSCME. In marked contrast to earlier relations between the two unions, the feeling was now one of harmony, and the convention closed happily.

A week after the convention Zander wrote to a friend: "I am writing President Green today asking how we should make application. It is our hope that this matter can be laid before the AFL executive council during its October meeting. It may be impossible for the council to act finally in October, but consideration of our problem at that time would undoubtedly speed final action."

In retrospect it seems apparent that Zander misread the power structure of the AFL by concentrating his letter-writing campaign on Green who, as a weak president, made few decisions. It can be speculated that had Zander directed his efforts at the real leaders—Dan Tobin of the Teamsters, Phillip Murray of the Steelworkers, John L. Lewis of the Mineworkers—he would have had an easier time obtaining the charter.

On October 8, 1936 Zander and AFSCME executive board member Frank C. Snyder went before the executive council of the AFL. The council had already heard the recommendations of AFGE, and after Zander and Snyder presented their case, it debated the question A vote was taken late in the day, and the

23

decision was to grant AFSCME a separate charter as a national union of state, county and municipal employees.

What had begun as a counterreaction to a political power play resulted in the creation of a new force in the American labor movement, one that over the four decades to come would have an enormous effect on the movement and on American society.

The first biennial convention of American Federation of State, County and Municipal Employees, Book-Cadillac Hotel, Detroit, Michigan. Sept. 17-19, 1936. (Zander, center foreground with hands folded; Garey wearing white shoes)

24

2.   The Thirties, a Time of Stunted Growth

*In our federation there is a strong interest in the
establishment of sound public administration, and
by working together, we as the international union
for state, county, and municipal employees can be a
tremendous force for good in the development of
public service.*

from the Souvenir Program,
AFSCME's Third International Convention
Atlanta, Georgia August 1938

This theme of public service patriotism hardly sounds
like the typical union rhetoric of the thirties. However, the
American Federation of State, County and Municipal Employees has always been in a special position in the American
labor movement. When the movement was militant and
aggressive, AFSCME was cautious and conservative; when the
movement would settle for a position of respectability, accepted as a compatible member of the establishment, AFSCME
would rise and fight for rights it had been denied.

The reasons for the union's early caution were both
external and internal. The external reasons had to do with
acceptance of unions and economic conditions.

The thirties was indeed a period when labor gained
stature through legislation (Norris-LaGuardia Act of 1932

25

and Wagner Act of 1935) and the election of Franklin D. Roosevelt. In *Labor Unions in America* (1964) John Herling wrote:

> An immediate effect of the Wagner Act was to encourage workers to join unions and to organize unions in areas where they do not exist. Only after this assurance of government support could union leaders overcome long-entrenched employer resistance. It was now the employers who found themselves struggling to adjust to government policies—not always an easy task.

But Herling was writing about trade and industrial unions, not public employee unions. At the same time that established unions were making headway as collective bargaining agents, public employee unions were feeling their way tentatively in an area where there were no patterns or precedents. Except for a few isolated cases, collective bargaining agreements in the public sector were nonexistent, and public employees had always been forbidden by law to strike.

The economy was still recovering from the depression, and public employees, traditionally low paid, were among the hardest hit by poverty. In *Hard Times* Studs Terkel quotes Elsa Ponselle, an elementary school principal in Chicago:

> I began to teach in December, 1930, and I was paid until June 1931. When we came back, the city had gone broke. We kept on teaching, of course. My father provided me with enough money to get by. But it was another thing for the men who were married and had children. . .

Internally AFSCME was inhibited in its dealings with management by its own makeup and the philosophy of its leaders, the membership consisting of many white-collar professionals not inclined toward militancy, some even feeling an anti-union bias.

A description of AFSCME's early membership is contained in a letter from Zander to AFL President Green in December 1936:

> In the jurisdiction granted to us nurses, physicians, research assistants, institutional attendants, matrons, clinical helpers, and other professionals are named specifically, and we are interested and are now busy organizing these workers. In fact, a large part of our membership at the present time is made up of state, county, and municipal institutional employees, including nurses, laboratory technicians, and other hospital professionals.

Growth in the early years of AFSCME was not easy, and the attitude that unionization was not a right of public employees persisted. As late as 1943 Zander was approaching the issue cautiously. He told a meeting of state employees in Kansas:

> We have been told that it was illegal for public officials to deal with their employees collectively, but the whole aspect of things in regard to that matter has changed with the extension of our organization. It has been stated publicly by some who were presumed to know that public officials could not bargain collectively with their employees, and enter into collective bargaining agreements. We now have a large number of agreements in effect and are prepared to defend their legality in the courts.

In regard to the right of public employees to strike, AFSCME's leadership felt it best to avoid the volatile issue entirely. So the union constitution made no reference to it. Instead the constitution was prefaced with a statement of goals and reflects an attitude of not viewing government as a necessary evil or even as opposition:

PREAMBLE

To improve and maintain the social and economic welfare of all employees of state, county, and municipal governments without regard to color, race, or creed, to promote efficiency in government, and to give clear evidence of recognition of our unity with organized labbor, we adopt this constitution. . .

ARTICLE II
OBJECTS AND METHODS

Section 1. The objects of this organization shall be:

a. To promote efficiency in public service generally.
b. To cooperate in giving efficient service to our respective jurisdictions.
c. To bring local organizations of state, county, and municipal employees into closer relationship so as to foster mutual cooperation.
d. To extend and uphold the principle of merit and fitness in public employment and to promote civil service legislation.
e. To establish and maintain a clearing-house of information and a research service for affiliated locals.
f. To foster and promote by education a new public attitude toward public administration.
g. To advance the general, social, and economic welfare of state, county, and municipal employees.
h. To promote organization of workers generally and of public employees in particular.

Section 2. The methods of obtaining the objects of this federation shall be by petitioning, by creating

28

and fostering sentiment favorable to proposed reforms, by cooperating with state and local officials, by promoting legislation, and by other lawful means.

The union simply was not militant, and what militancy did exist was of a minority, not tolerated for long. For example, a number of locals made up mainly of welfare caseworkers had split off in 1937 to form the State, County, and Municipal Workers of America, SCMWA. Led by one-time AFSCME executive board member Abraham Flaxer and Secretary-Treasurer David Kanes, this group of 5,000 members, many Communists among them, affiliated with the CIO.

Zander and Gordon W. Chapman, Kanes' replacement as secretary-treasurer, were regularly reelected to union leadership. Both were dedicated to the civil service system, and neither would attempt too much too soon and risk gains already achieved. As state employees they also favored the tactic of passing or strengthening civil service laws and merit systems which could in the foreseeable future take the place of such drastic measures as strikes.

Throughout the membership white-collar professionals were the dominating force, and they remained so for the first quarter century of the union's existence. Later, when county and municipal locals began to join in increasing numbers and the big city locals and councils realized their own strength, the balance would shift. But the changes in attitude that shift would create were years away in both time and philosophy from the public employee unionism of the late 1930s.

Arnold Zander was and is an intellectual. He received a Ph.D. in Public Administration from the University of Wisconsin before he entered the American labor movement, and he returned to Wisconsin to teach after leaving it. His father was an active Socialist, and Arnold used to carry a soapbox around for his father to stand on when making Sunday speeches about the danger of unfettered capitalism.

When Arnold was a child, the Zander household was filled with exciting guests, national figures of the day.

The early socialist influence, tempered by academic training, made Zander feel at home in a state under the progressive leadership of LaFollette, a state widely considered to be a social laboratory and a state which fostered one of the first civil service systems, with which Zander was associated from the very beginning of his career.

In line with the notion that only the best should serve the state, Zander carried his civil service beliefs into his union philosophy, assuming that AFSCME's membership was better educated than the average union membership and should act accordingly. Zander's method was cooperation and quiet negotiation, and he would never be one to pound on a bargaining table or give a fiery organizational speech. Emotional outbursts were considered a dangerous luxury that his union simply could not afford and did not fit his image of the union's membership or suit his own temperament as a Ph.D., Christian Scientist and responsible labor leader.

Joseph Ames, a long-time AFSCME official who served as secretary-treasurer of the union for six years and today is chairman of the union's judicial panel, confirms that Zander's philosophy was based on a belief that his membership was "a cut above the average union membership." But Ames, a leader in the rebellion that would later unseat Zander, feels this philosophy had "catastrophic effects on the structure of the union." In Ames' view, Zander felt the rank and file membership was capable of handling its problems without professional assistance. "Consequently," says Ames, "he deliberately developed a structure that was (1) severely underfinanced and (2) consisted mainly of small locals, each expected to manage its own problems."

Given the benefit of historical perspective, it appears that public employee unionism at the time of the formation of AFSCME was an idea whose time had almost come but not quite, and the thought that public workers could behave like their

The early founders of AFSCME, from left to right, Chapman, Garey and
Zander, at convention in 1952

counterparts in industry was out of the question. Thus the early years, although active and eventful, represented a waiting period characterized by careful organization, nonmilitancy and a stress on professionalism.

In the first few years new membership depended as much on acquisition of existing locals as on the organization of new ones. At the time there were numerous small and a few large public employee organizations around the country. The AFL provided Zander with lists of directly affiliated locals, and he traveled as much as the limited budget allowed, exhorting these unions to come aboard.

By the end of 1936, after three months of existence, the membership of AFSCME, according to per capita tax figures, was 9,737. In 1937 the number was 13,259. In 1946, after the union's first decade, membership stood at slightly more than 73,000.

White-collar professionals continued to dominate the membership for the first 25 years of the union's existence, and leadership was almost entirely in the hands of bureaucrats. While blue-collar workers, members of a state highway department local, for example, were joining in increasing numbers, their voice in union business and internal political issues was much more muted than it was in later years.

In 1946 the AFSCME research department provided a European publication with information that contained a description of membership:

> *The Structure and Importance*
> *of the A.F.S.C. and M.E.*
>
> The A.F.S.C. and M.E. includes in its ranks every type of state, county, and municipal employee—manual and white-collar alike—with the exception of those employees over whom jurisdiction had been granted previously to other national and international unions. . .
> . . .A.F.S.C. and M.E. (has) jurisdiction over the following employees of state, county and municipal

32

governments: clerical, secretarial, administrative, and fiscal services; sub-professional services, such as agricultural, bacteriological, biological, and chemical aides; clinical helpers and library assistants; professional services such as accountants, actuaries, probation and parole officers, bacteriologists, chemists, geologists, nurses, physicians, law clerks, librarians, and research assistants; inspectional and investigational services, such as legal investigators, sealers of weights and measures, securities examiners, commodity and farm produce inspectors, food inspectors; and woman and child labor inspectors; and general groups such as institutional farm employees, gardeners, herdsmen, conservation workers, forest rangers, institutional attendants, matrons, prison guards, and jail keepers.

It would not be right to say that by 1946 the union membership was 73,000 *strong,* for despite its growth in numbers, AFSCME was anything but strong. It was plagued by problems that most industrial unions had overcome or never encountered, problems having to do with (1) the relationship of members and the union; (2) practices and attitudes of public employers; and (3) a shaky financial condition.

A basic principle of the union was the independence of an individual member, local or council. An AFSCME member was free to quit at any time, and in most cases he was not inhibited by the argument that he owed his job to the union. So as a rule, if he didn't like the union, he didn't try to change it, he just left.

In one sense this enabled the union to deal from a position of strength, for an employer realized his workers, having signed up voluntarily with AFSCME, were quite possibly more dedicated than some unionists.

On the other hand independence was a burden for the leadership which lacked control not only over individual members but over autonomous locals as well. As an early union publication explained:

> The responsibility for organization is divided between local unions and international headquarters. It is the responsibility of local unions to expand organization within their jurisdiction with the goal of getting 100% membership. International headquarters is charged with the responsibility of organizing new locals. Local unions should also strive to improve standards of pay and working conditions of employees within their membership.

One reason for local independence was the union's financial position. The international staff, headquartered in Madison, Wisconsin, was small, and it could neither afford to work in the field nor bring local leaders to headquarters for training.

Perhaps the clearest indication of the limitations placed on the work of international headquarters is that the per capita tax, the amount of each member's $2.00 monthly dues that went to headquarters, was at that time 35 cents. The union's basic principle of local autonomy made it difficult for the national union to convince the membership that it should turn over a larger portion of its dues. Throughout Zander's presidency the union was in financial straits. As late as 1962 a convention fight centered on Zander's unsuccessful attempt to raise the per capita tax from 65 cents to a dollar.

It was also true in the early years that officials of state, county and local governments were by no means convinced they had to accept the union as a voice in deciding policies concerning wages, hours and working conditions. AFSCME's credibility with the boss was difficult to achieve.

Wurf: The Early Years

The most important thing I can say about that early era is that nobody, but nobody, took seriously the possibility of collective bargaining in public service. Affiliation with the labor movement was premised on the theory that labor was a good ally for the purpose of beefing up the civil service system through legislation or supporting a local situation by getting a city council to act. The proud boast at one of the first conventions I attended was that the union got civil service laws passed in 20 states.

Our union didn't struggle with collective bargaining until the young turks, as Zander called us, came along. I came in 1948, and the other young turks came in the '50s, and we were the guys who brought the concept that government is no different than industry. We had a hard time selling it because of this civil service emphasis, so many people mistakenly believing that one weakened the other when exactly the opposite is true. Job security was the raison d'etre rather than the salvation of the worker. There was a depression psychology in the union that lasted until quite recently, until my election, I suppose.

There is a big thing I would immodestly point out: that it was we in New York who persuaded Mayor Wagner to issue an executive order that began real collective bargaining in New York and that later influenced the Kennedy order which revolutionized public service in America.

We didn't just revolutionize the labor-management relationship. We brought about changes in the entire labor movement, changes in society, changes in the politics of cities and states, changes in attitudes, the patronage system, and in many places—in Pennsylvania as recently as 1972—we revolutionized the relationships of hundreds of thousands of people.

All of these things stemmed from efforts that originated in New York. New York is really the incubator. . . .

Signs of progress: Zander with Sen. Robert F. Wagner of New York.
They were principal speakers at the council of New York City local
unions in 1944

3. Then Came Growth, and With It Stability

The AFSCME convention of 1946 was the first in six years, since none could be held during World War II, and it came at a time when the union had begun to experience a slowdown in growth.

There were several reasons for the lag:

- With the country in an inflationary mood workers were lured away from public employment by the higher pay private business offered.
- Other unions coveted the ranks of public workers and began to raid AFSCME. The Teamsters were particularly adept at sporadic raids, a practice they continue today.
- As always, AFSCME was plagued by a lack of money for organizational purposes.
- The AFL and CIO had not yet merged, and some public employee locals shunned AFSCME, for they preferred a CIO affiliation.
- Government officials still had not accepted the idea of public employee unions.
- The union hadn't been able to prove itself as a consistently effective vehicle for advancing the well-being of its members.

The historical resistance to extending the principles of the trade union movement to public unions was not easily overcome, nor has it by any means been eliminated today. Most public employers in the forties and fifties had a clear and in some cases fond memory of a 1937 letter written by President Roosevelt in which he said:

> All government employees should recognize that collective bargaining, as usually understood, cannot be transplanted into the public service . . . Militant tactics have no place in the functions of any organization of government employees. . . Since their services have to do with the functioning of government, a strike of government employees manifests nothing less than an attempt on their part to prevent or obstruct the operations of government until their demands are satisfied. Such actions looking toward the paralysis of government by those who have sworn to support it is unthinkable and intolerable.

Another factor, explained by Zander's former chief aide, Leo Kramer, in his book, *Labor's Paradox,* was the influence of a series of legal briefs prepared by Charles S. Rhyne, then general counsel for the National Institute of Municipal Law Officers, which were used as guides by the legal departments of most cities. Kramer summarized their impact: "The philosophical bias of the reports was that it was undesirable for a city to deal with a union of its employees."

Postwar inflation created jobs up and down the economic ladder but also emphasized to public workers their second class status, as private industry awarded inferior ability with higher pay.

The reaction was "general unrest throughout the country among local government employees," according to a review of 1946 found in a chronology of unionism in public employment, written in 1970 by Larry Rogin, then coordinator of staff training at AFSCME. Rogin continued:

> There were strikes of city employees in San Francisco, Detroit, Cleveland, Houston, and Niagara Falls, Portland, Maine and a number of other cities. Most of the strikes involved sanitation and public works departments, but transit and city hall employees were also involved. In Rochester, New York, both AFL and CIO unions rallied behind a city employee strike caused by the discharge of those who had tried to form a union. The right to organize was established. There were strikes of state employees in Ohio and other states.

In addition, there were 16 teacher strikes in 1946.

Reaction to the discontent was quick. In 1946 Virginia denied recognition to public employee unions and refused to negotiate with them, and Virginia's employees were forbidden to join a union that claimed the right to strike. The next year the Supreme Court of Ohio declared that checkoff of union dues was illegal for public employees.

Michigan passed the Hutcheson Act in 1947, stipulating penalties for striking public workers, although there was a provision for mediation in public employee disputes. New York passed the Condon-Wadlin Act, outlawing public employee strikes and setting penalties for strikers.

Concessions to public employee unions were few. Two federal actions had given them a boost, but they applied only to federal employees. Congress amended the Social Security Act to require states to protect by a merit system all employees in departments that received Social Security grant-in-aid funds, and in 1940 the Civil Service Commission established mandatory grievance procedures for federal employees.

Laws that would penalize striking public workers were passed in eight states by the end of 1947, the year Congress passed the Taft-Hartley Act. Designed to restrict labor unions in private industry, Taft-Hartley included a no-strike clause

39

for federal employees.

A present AFSCME staff member, Al Bilik, who was hired by Zander in 1950 as a field organizer, reflected on the attitude toward public workers in a law journal article in 1970:

> There appears to be generally in the United States a material and psychological need to harp on the uniqueness of public employment. The American people have throughout our history tended to view government as a detached "them" institution, an institution that has "taken" from the people more than it has "given." From the tax collectors of George III to the tax collectors of the modern day, government employees have enjoyed a special status in American life.

Despite the opposition and negative climate for public employee unions in the forties, there were big breakthroughs in the fifties, although changes in attitude—by both employees and employers—were gradual. In every year but 1951, when the Korean War was raging, there were membership gains, and with the merger of the AFL and CIO the rolls were pushed over the 100,000 mark.

The merger wasn't the only reason for the surge in membership. Five other important ones were:

1) Acceptance of the checkoff system by employers in which they pay a worker's dues directly to the union. Checkoff, which reduces turnover, was probably the most significant growth factor.

2) A merger in 1956 between AFSCME and the 30,000 member Government and Civic Employees Organizing Committee.

3) Inability of state and local governments to thwart the right of public workers to organize.

4) AFSCME locals and councils were deemphasizing good government as a primary goal in favor of

improving the rights of members through collective bargaining.

5) The locals and councils were beginning to win important concessions at the state, county and municipal level.

The growth pattern of the fifties was positive progress for which Zander deserves due credit, but signs of militancy no doubt gave the president pause. Zander well understood that the traditional bias against public employee unionism would take a long time subsiding, and he tried to deal with it by stressing the importance of promoting good government, even though some leaders of locals and councils were taking a more militant tack. Zander felt it was foolhardy to resort to the rhetoric of trade unionism with public managers who were paternalistic to their employees and antagonistic to their unions.

Zander was not at heart a trade unionist. His training and background made him an advocate of the merit system and civil service. Past and present union officials alike speak of Zander's belief that the public employee—especially the white-collar employee—was inherently superior to the trade union member because he had proven his ability on a competitive written examination. Given this superiority, the argument runs, he has less need for collective bargaining and the right to strike.

There are some, however, who feel this view is unfair to Zander, who was, they claim, only acting pragmatically because he knew he was handicapped when negotiating with public officials who had the power of legal restrictions against collective bargaining and the right to strike. At any rate, it is clear that Zander believed that public employees served the common good of the state, and even by 1958, when he had been speaking openly about collective bargaining for several years, the old stress on service remained, as shown in an article published by the union:

41

While the union's general organizing efforts face such problems as public employer opposition, an absence of stated rights for public employees, heavy turnover, the fear instilled by long years of political patronage, and high costs, special problems are raised by the organization of white collar workers. The latter often feel close to management or too "professional" to join a union.

AFSCME's approach to these workers is to emphasize the benefits won by blue collar workers and white collar workers alike through organization. Professional employees, the union adds, have the same need for collective bargaining on rates of pay and working conditions as do other workers. In addition, AFSCME stresses to all categories of employees its goal of improving service to the community by enabling the public work force to function under the best conditions. This appeal strikes a particularly responsive note, probably indicating a generalized need for recognition of the social contribution made by the individual worker.

By 1958 Zander had served the cause of public employee unionism in one form or another for over a quarter century. He had been the only president of AFSCME, challenged for office just one time, and his executive board, though querulous over little matters, rarely gave him serious opposition when he proposed a major action that required its approval.

Although the late forties and early fifties had been a difficult period for public employee unions, Zander was in complete control of AFSCME. His strength was based on twenty years of careful stewardship, gathering new membership at a time when most state and local officials felt a worker should consider it a privilege to work for government.

Zander seemed so entrenched in 1958 that it would have been implausible to suggest that within a year there would be serious internal problems within AFSCME, or that in six years

Zander would be fighting a losing battle to stay in power. The revolution that was to spread swiftly through the movement is best understood in light of two developments. One is the change in attitude of the membership toward trade union practices; the other is the emergence of strong, younger leaders.

At the time of the AFL-CIO merger in 1955 Zander's strength lay in the loyalty of numerous small locals, most of which were controlled by state white-collar employees and which had an equal role with the fewer large city locals and councils. For the most part organizing had been done in smaller cities and rural areas. Many officials of the union believe that big cities, with certain exceptions, were purposely ignored because they presented more problems than the underfinanced union could tackle. As one former organizer put it, not without bitterness, "Look at the official photographs of those early conventions, 1948, '50, '52, and so on, and all you see is the same square-faced, crewcut, hayseed, blue-eyed Norwegian, state-level white collar worker from Minnesota."

Al Bilik, who in 1950 graduated from the first class of organizers trained by the union, has characterized Zander's attitude in the early fifties:

> Arnold Zander was comfortable with the rural membership and quite satisfied with leaving the big cities alone. In 1950 we had 80,000 members but the major metropolitan areas were virtually untouched. Certainly there were difficulties with organizing the cities, but their strong labor movements and the city manager system provided cushion, yet Zander stayed away from them despite this because of his philosophical background, and also, in my opinion, because they could represent a threat to his power.

As the son of a populist-socialist Zander was opposed to the machine politics of large cities, and he shunned

43

metropolitan centers until it was impossible to do so any longer. Whether he realized it or not, the booming membership rise in big city locals and councils was to bring about his eventual loss of power.

All through the fifties there were clear signs that the attitude of the membership was changing, that the trend toward militancy and power for the public worker was moving relentlessly forward. In 1950 the international convention had heard a report of the executive board that pointed out the importance of checkoff and exhorted the membership to work for its expansion. But according to Larry Rogin, "Many of the larger locals had already won dues deduction, sometimes as part of a working agreement. The union began to press for governmental action, including legislation where necessary, authorizing this practice."

By 1954 the membership was markedly more interested in adopting some of the basic tenets of trade unionism. Early in the year New York City employees were granted the right, based on an executive order from the mayor, to join unions. The order, in large part the result of AFSCME's efforts, required the city departments to deal with the unions.

The New York victory and other negotiating successes had led to an instruction to union officers at the 1954 convention to intensify their efforts to obtain collective bargaining agreements. There was also a strong expression of support for more efforts to assure passage of state collective bargaining laws for public workers.

As large city locals became affiliated with AFSCME, bringing with them thousands of new members representing a broader base of public employment, the men who headed these groups became more influential. In time they were to become powerful, but then the union's constitution contained a voting representation system that limited the power of larger locals and councils.

It had always been Zander's view that strength should come from a variety of small locals in numerous areas of the

44

country, rather than the powerful large councils. Attempts to change the voting representation that had been started in 1950 had begun to succeed in 1954. Acceding to demands of the larger blocs, the convention that year changed the voting system, effective 1956, to provide that every local under 100 members would get one vote, and every additional 100 members up to 1,000 one more vote per hundred; an additional vote would be granted for every 200 members up to 2,000, another vote for every 300 up to 2,900, another vote for every 400 up to 4,100 members, and one vote for each additional 500 members above 4,100.

In 1956 merger with the 30,000 member Government and Civic Employees Organizing Committee gave added impetus to the reform movement. GCEOC leaders tended to be aggressive and militant with employers, and Al Bilik remembers being surprised to learn that GCEOC already had a number of written agreements with cities such as Louisville.

New AFSCME members joined a union dominated by Zander, and the younger aggressors were beginning to stir. The names of some would be heard when the union entered the '60s: Ames of St. Louis, Schut of Washington state, Bilik of Cincinnati, Hastings, Gotbaum and Morgan of the international staff and Wurf of New York.

The forces that would try to contain the uprising were led by Zander, Secretary-Treasurer Chapman, William McEntee, director of the Philadelphia council, and Leo Kramer, a young organizer hired by Zander in 1949. Kramer soon became a Zander favorite, was named to the staff of international headquarters and by 1958 was called by Zander, "an extension of my desk."

In the late fifties Wurf was assigned as an international staffer to Council 37 in New York, a strong organization in terms of growth and benefits thanks to Wurf's talent for leadership. Zander had hired Wurf in March 1948, and over the years their professional relationship deepened, was even friendly despite character contrasts: Zander, the Christian

45

Scientist who had come from academia and the Wisconsin civil service system; Wurf, the profane Jew from a New York milieu of stab in the back machinations, a street organizer who had his own claim to intellectualism.

Both men leaned to socialism, but Zander learned it at home where, in the comfort of friendly conversation, distinctions became blurred. To Wurf being a Socialist was less comfortable, for in New York he not only had to fight the Communists, whom he despised, he also had to buck the bias that socialism and communism were kindred philosophies, if not one and the same.

There are various views on just how deep the Zander-Wurf relationship was. Today Wurf says, "We were never what you'd call intimate," although others mention a father-son relationship. Bilik suggests that Wurf felt a combination of admiration and envy for Zander, but he discounts the idea of real intimacy.

Wurf: Agitator without a Cause

I grew up in New York in the '30s and '40s and when I was going to school and college I felt strongly about the need for drastic change in the economic and political system. I was outraged by the degree of influence the Communists had on our small, liberal circle. They were inconsistent, hypocritical—they always were looking elsewhere for direction. My reaction to them was very strong. I remember making speeches in Brighton Beach, the neighborhood in which I was brought up, where there were probably more Communists in a square mile than any place in the United States. Our socialist movement was very small, and as if we didn't have enough trouble with the Communists, we had to take on the Trotskyites as well. We fought the Fascists too—down in Columbus Circle where they would stand on soap boxes denouncing Jews and praising the regimes in Italy and Germany. But the police were always there, and the best we could do was ask provocative questions.

46

But I felt impotent, and I came to the conclusion that to have an impact on the system, we needed a mechanism that could change it, although I had few illusions that I would or could.

A fellow Socialist named Max Segal fixed me up with a job as a cafeteria cashier and busboy, and I helped him organize Local 448, Food Checkers and Cashiers Union of the Hotel and Restaurant Employees.

Cafeterias were big business in those days, because you could get food cheap and you could hang around and talk. They had a useful place in society, like the coffee houses in Europe.

Max Segal was terribly decent, terribly moral but not very ambitious. Here was this little union, struggling along, and a great chance comes to organize the Garden Cafeteria, which was on the corner where the Jewish Daily Forward was located on the lower east side of New York. I took the position we could get a contract with the Garden because it was in a neighborhood of people—left wing, right wing, Social Democrat, Trotskyite, Orthodox Jew—who wouldn't cross a picket line. But another guy who had joined our staff, Jimmy Landau, gave Segal a thousand reasons why we couldn't get a contract.

We argued for two days, and I finally persuaded Max to get a couple of pieces of cardboard, and we started picketing the Garden Cafeteria, whereupon the Commie leader of Local 302 that represented the cafeteria's cooks, countermen, busboys and dishwashers came along and and said, "What the hell is going on?"

I told him our union had jurisdiction over the cashiers. He said, "The hell you do," and I suggested we argue it out some other place.

The Commie took me for a cup of coffee, and we talked, and he learned I was a Social Democrat, which is a very bad thing to an old time Stalinist.

He smelled a plot to run him out of the area, but he said, "I don't know what the hell you're doing, Jerry, I don't know

47

what this is all about, and although I'll probably regret it, I'm going to shut the joint down." And he did, and when the owner came out screaming he had a deal with a guy named Landau, I told him in my own inhibited way that if he had a deal with Landau, he could go tell all about his deal to Tom Dewey, the district attorney in New York, and see if he'd enforce it.

In any event, we got rid of Landau, we organized the Garden Cafeteria cashiers and I emerged as a voice of power in the local. Segal got bored with not being able to make a living or else his wife put the heat on him, but he went into the hardware business, and Wurf had his own union. I joined the Brooklyn joint board and became a noisy opponent of the Commies and the underworld guys who controlled some of the locals of the Hotel and Restaurant Employees, and, of course, they greeted me like a dose of clap.

Then my union was merged with a Brooklyn local, which became known as Local 325, Cooks, Countermen, Soda Dispensers, Cashiers and Assistants Union, affiliated with the Hotel and Restaurant Employees International. I was supposed to administer a welfare fund, but I had great difficulty. The other union officials were fearful I might upset their situations. They wanted our Cashiers local, but some of them would have liked to eliminate me. Eventually they fired me as welfare administrator, figuring I'd get lost.

I was articulate. I was concerned. But I guess I was dumb. I wasn't one of the boys, and I raised questions about union administration, financial statements and the democratic process, so pretty soon they sent me running. I suppose they figured that with my education I wouldn't hang around as a rank-and-filer.

I was a professional agitator without a cause. There was no alternative but to stand outside the union hiring hall and insist I get a day's work. Eventually I'd be sent out as a cashier, but the boss had a right to fire me within the first hour. After I was fired a few times, it was clear I wasn't going to make that first hour, and I began to suspect a conspiracy.

48

So when it happened again, as the boss was discharging me I said, "I want to tell you something, boss." I said, "I think you got a phone call to do this, because you know I'm a decent union man, and I'm being run out of the union. But I'm not going to leave the union, you sonofabirch, and the day will come when I'm a union official, and I want you to know you're going to have the best paying contract we got, that is if you're still in business."

Well, that had its effect, and a few days later I was sitting in the Concord Cafeteria in Brooklyn where I knew both the bosses and the workers. The boss said, "Do you want to go to work, Jerry?" And I said, "I haven't got a ticket," meaning the ticket the union handed out like a license to work.

Then the shop steward, a man of considerable stature in a joint like that, came over and said, "Of course you can go to work, Jerry, old militant, great tosser of plates on picket lines." I became a relief man.

I'd been working in the Concord about a week when a couple of officials of 325 walked over to me and asked who gave me permission to work and where was my ticket. I said I didn't have a ticket, but I figured the union knew I needed work, and that every time I got a ticket and my turn came up, the union told the boss to knock me off.

They ordered me from behind the counter, and while I was counting the money and the cigars and cigarettes, the shop steward came by and demanded to know what was going on. "Jerry doesn't believe in the system," said one union official. "He has violated the most basic rules and is due to come up on charges, so I'm hauling him off this job. The goddamn boss is lucky we don't shut him down."

The steward countered: "I know Jerry is on the blacklist, but I don't give a damn about union politics. I do my day's work and go home. But I don't like this kind of stuff. Unions are supposed to help people, not hurt them. Matter of fact, the shop works well with him here, so why don't you guys knock it off."

Well, with that every last guy in the place walked off his

49

station. They were going to strike against the goddamn union unless I was put back to work. It was one of the greatest moments of my life.

By the late fifties AFSCME had been transformed from a union protective of civil servants pledged to good government to a sleeping giant of almost 180,000 members. And no longer were those members, advocates of equal rights for public employees, satisfied with quiet deals in city managers' offices. They were ready to take to the streets.

It was at this time that Col. Garey, one of the founders of AFSCME, left the union. He attended the 1960 convention, though he was all but officially retired. The events of that meeting must have shocked him, for there was warfare on the floor, secret caucuses and bitter denunciations.

Al Bilik, who describes the Colonel simply as "a great man," says he was always ideologically opposed to collective bargaining and worried about adopting the practices of trade unionism in the public sector. At the time of his retirement that is exactly where the union was headed.

Wurf: Going to Work for AFSCME

I was looking for a job in the late forties, and I happened to be at a Workers Defense League lunch where Zander was sitting at the head table. Zander had just taken over a dissident union of transit workers that was fighting Mike Quill's Transport Workers Union, and Zander had a mandate from William Green to try to take the workers away from the TWU. The TWU was a CIO union, Mike Quill was regarded as a Communist, and both were anathemas to the AFL. I got into a discussion with Zander, the result of which was he hired me as a $60 a week organizer. I guess I inherited the mandate to put Quill out of business, which was a little like trying to melt an iceberg with a match.

When the AFL Labor Council started rounding up workers to scab in the event the subways were struck by the CIO—a

50

demonstration of labor's loyalty to the political mother—I deplored the whole process. I let Zander know I didn't like Commies and I didn't like Quill. Neither did I like the mayor, nor the central body, but most especially I didn't like being a scab hunter. So I asked to quit, at which point I was summoned to Madison to speak with his royal imperial highness.

I stayed with Zander even though I was treated with some contempt by the rest of the labor movement in New York. First I needed a job since I knew I was through with the Hotel and Restaurant Employees, and I didn't really want to be a cashier. Second, I began to believe after a while that the public worker movement was one that might be changed; it was susceptible to new ideas.

I was also gratified that Zander would accept a rebel, which I was in the sense that I wouldn't accept the status quo, and that he would appreciate my loyalty while tolerating my independence.

In my early years with the union I did some really rough things to help Zander keep control of conventions. I was willing to destroy my own credibility by manipulating on his behalf. I don't think I ever violated decency, but I came damn close.

There were many qualities of Zander's that appalled me: his obsequious posturing to the AFL inner circle leadership, his acceptance of hospitality from vendors, his naive willingness to accept participation in the union by real Neanderthals.

Yet there I was. I had renounced my radicalism, and I was trying to get involved in a trade union movement which I thought could have an impact on the system. Zander showed allegiance to the things I believed in: consumer cooperation, housing programs, peace. He admired Eugene Debs, as I did, and he admitted that Norman Thomas was probably the clearest voice of our time.

I was looking for somebody to follow. A guy who had polio as a kid and is always the last to be picked when they

51

choose up sides for baseball, who can't swim as well as other kids or run as fast or play punch ball—is the kind of guy who looks for heroes. He may not be insensitive to their flaws, but he is willing to rationalize.

Jerry Wurf at the 1954 convention in Chicago

Joe Ames at the 1954 convention in Chicago

4.   Enter an Emerging New Leadership

The eleventh biennial convention of the American Federation of State, County and Municipal Employees opened at 10:00 a.m. on Monday, April 28, 1958 in Long Beach, California. Monsignor Dolan of St. Anthony's church in that city began his invocation by praying: "We invoke Thy blessing, Oh Lord, on the members of this great and far-reaching organization of labor gathered here for serious deliberation, to discuss the many and vexing problems that so intimately touch them as responsible citizens in their service to the different departments of government in this favored land."

The good father was right on the mark, albeit unintentionally, in his reference to "many and vexing problems," though he was speaking of external problems. In 1958, however, the union was plagued with a number of internal problems that caused the eventual clash between Zander's administration and the growing number of young dissidents. How great was the dissatisfaction felt by certain segments of the membership would not be seen until the next convention, but in 1958 there were several clashes on the floor that portended the acrimony of the '60s.

In his opening address Arnold Zander lost little time getting to the point of trouble in the union:

> I wish that I could merely dwell on these successes that we have had, and to say to you that we

have been as one, that we have shared whatever sense of satisfaction we could get out of this, and that we have gloried together in being known throughout the land as a highly respected and the most rapidly-growing union in the movement.

I must, however, speak to evil. I address myself to it, briefly, I hope. I address myself to evil, not to evildoers, to those who have not been able to get satisfaction from the record which has been established, but who seem instead to be irked by success; who would, it seems, be much more satisfied if we had fallen on our faces and come to you with a report of failure. This is not a satisfying or pleasant task, but one I am advised I must undertake.

Zander was referring to an action he considered a serious breach of good union manners and procedures. Several members had objected to the relatively new practice of allowing paid international representatives to come to the convention and vote as delegates of locals or councils. They had taken the matter directly to AFL-CIO President George Meany by asking him to intercede. Meany wanted no part of the game and sent the ball back with an obvious rebuke: "I do not gather from your letter that this practice is in violation of the international's constitution."

Zander continued:

One would think that might put the matter at rest. But when the obvious intent is to smear, then there is no stopping. And so it seems, one reaches down inside himself and comes up with venom and bile to spew out against his organization, and yours and mine. But he can't reach it. The union is still white and unsullied. It can't be tarnished in this way.

Zander then revealed that the members who had written Meany had tried another tack:

54

A delegate sitting on the floor of this convention recently inserted in the public press charges against the international union and its officers . . . .

Two long columns, declaring in public print that along with the Teamsters and the Bakery Workers and these unions which have been disciplined out of the movement, this union has engaged in identically the same practices. And I say this is evil, and this is a lie. I am calling no one a liar. I am saying this is a lie. He who perpetrated this may answer for himself.

I declare to you, and as God may be my witness, there is no single act which we have performed in the 20 some years during which we have devoted ourselves to the service of this union, which is to our knowledge corrupt or inimical—or use any other words of the constitution—as charged by a delegate, in public prints, without even the decency or the courtesy of providing us a copy, either before or after the act.

It is this kind of evil to which I address myself.

Zander's attack on "evil" shocked some of the delegates, but those who knew him well were familiar with his inclination to view strong opposition as evil. This inclination would grow to an emotional peak by 1964.

There were a few more examples of "evil" during the 1958 convention. The members who had written George Meany offered an amendment stating that no paid representative could act as a delegate for locals other than his own. There were three other heated debates on internal union matters, and although Zander won all four fights, it was a Pyrrhic victory, for the membership could see that the internal trouble was real. Argument on the floor frequently went beyond the point of polite disagreement, as when Father Albert Blatz, a Catholic priest who was a delegate from Minnesota and part of the group Zander sought to label "evil," stood up to oppose a motion to abolish the post of administrative vice-president, a position created for Milton Murray, head of GCEOC, when it merged with AFSCME.

As far as the issue is involved, I think it is, should we or should we not continue an office. I don't think we are speaking about the man who is in it—just the office, apart from the man.

Now I have heard it said that this is getting too cumbersome, we are getting too many people up at the top and no one down below . . . .

I don't think we can have too many up there . . . .

I would like to see enough people at the top so that I know one man isn't going to take the reins in his mouth and take off any way he wants to go. And I am not afraid of an extra man up there. I get the feeling, as I sit here—President Zander has quoted Shakespeare. Maybe we can quote a little Shakespeare, and I was reminded several times yesterday and today of a quote—I think it's accurate—"Methinks the gentleman doth protest too much."
[Applause]

I don't know what we are afraid of. I listened to a speech yesterday saying that during the last two years we have made the best progress we have ever made. This was credited to two factors: One reason given was because our per capita tax was increased. Another reason that was given was because we have been able to enter into special arrangements. I had a very long and thorough course in logic, and this is the funniest logic I have ever heard. If we are going to use that kind of logic, the progress was made when we had this administrative vice-president position, and therefore we had better keep it . . . .

I have heard people tell me this position must be eliminated. I have not heard one good, constructive reason why. [Applause]

The real reason the position was to be abolished was that Zander wanted as little company as possible at the top of the union. This was not a stand Zander had taken simply because he saw possible opposition to his leadership, but one in which he had been perfectly consistent from the very beginning. As early as 1937 Zander had opposed the concept of an elected secretary-treasurer (which the union had adopted from the constitution of the American Federation of Government Employees) because he felt that a better model for his union was that of the European trade unions in which there was only one elected full-time administrative officer. Throughout the early years of the union he resisted, on an ideological basis, the growing power of the office of secretary-treasurer, preferring a single strong executive and an administrative staff, with the secretary-treasurer's role confined to what he called in 1937 "a book-keeper's function."

This attitude was not in keeping with the practice within the American trade union movement, although, as Zander well knew, in many of the largest unions in this country the real power was held by one man.

As the rift in the union widened over the next six years, this issue of one man rule would be raised again and again.

The next flareup on the floor of the '58 convention came when an amendment was proposed to the constitution to clarify the situation known as special arrangements, agreements by which international headquarters would provide staff and money for the operation of a local or council which had strong possibilities for organization but was not able to realize them for reasons of underfinancing or understaffing. Once the local or council could stand on its own feet, it would regain control of its jurisdiction.

Originally the plan had worked well, but as the incidence of special arrangements grew, there were complaints that they were being used to extend the international's control over local jurisdictions. To rectify the situation a number of delegates had proposed an amendment that would define guidelines for special arrangements. After studying the proposal the Committee of Laws recommended nonconcurrence, meaning it opposed the amendment.

The amendment did not pass, but several strong opinions were voiced during the debate. Delegate Leo Bernat of Local 22 in Minnesota was an early speaker in favor of the measure. After relating how eager his local had been to enter into a special arrangement on the strength of promises made by the international, he recounted the problems that had arisen, problems he clearly characterized as stemming from bad faith on the part of the parent body. Bernat's statement was lengthy.

> PRESIDENT ZANDER [Interrupting]: Delegate Bernat, you have run over your time. Will you please conclude?
>
> DELEGAGE BERNAT: In a very brief statement, the purposes of the special arrangement we find good and laudable and desirable. But the particular language of this provision allows, as in the last sentence or two, for participation in local events and in council events by the international, and it's unilateral. You go in in a joint arrangement, and you cannot terminate it except at the will of the international in the general circumstances. And we find that this unilateral arrangement of getting out of it is unsatisfactory. And so what we wanted to do was to reduce the wording to just allow for the arrangement without the specifics. [Applause]

Not everyone was as worked up about special arrangements as Bernat. A New York delegate objected to remarks that President Zander was not being fair.

> There has been no attempt to stifle discussion here. My complaint about the manner in which President Zander administers the chair is that he is

58

bending over backwards in an effort to be fair, so fair that it doesn't look as if I will ever get back to New York by the end of May. [Applause]

A few other delegates spoke in favor of special arrangements, and then Bernat attempted to speak again. When he was ruled out of order by the chair and shouted down repeatedly, it was apparent that this was not the unified, orderly convention the AFSCME membership was used to.

The convention then turned to an issue capable of changing the power structure of the union: should international vice-presidents be elected regionally or at large, as they always had been. The vice-presidents made up the union's executive board, and under Zander's administration their home base was incidental to their election, since the 11 highest vote-getters from anywhere were elected. It was contended that the executive board had come to resemble a rubber stamp for Zander.

The debate over the election of vice-presidents was in great part inspired by the issue of regional vs. national dominance, also demonstrated by concern at the '58 convention over the growing number of international representatives sent to work in the field. Some members feared the practice could threaten their autonomy and felt if the vice-presidents were elected regionally, there would be less likelihood the international would try to control local affairs.

The sides were still to be divided over regionalism, and they did not correspond to forces opposed to or supporting the Zander administration. Although it had been debated in other forms before, the regionalism issue was relatively new in 1958, and minds were still being made up. Delegates who opposed it vigorously would change their position in the next few years.

On the last day of the convention, in the midst of a number of routine resolutions, Minnesota's Council 6 offered a resolution that took but a few moments to pass. In hindsight it may have been more significant that anyone realized.

VICE-PRESIDENT CLARK: Resolution 31 deals with Public Employees Week.

". . . BE IT RESOLVED: That the name of 'Public Servants Week' be changed to 'Public Employees Week.' "

Submitted by: Albert B. Blatz, President
Florence Palm, Secretary
Minnesota Council of State Employees 6

Later that day Zander gave his closing remarks and included a strong pitch for an increase in the per capita tax, promising to bring it up before the 1960 convention in Philadelphia. In part of his address he also made an interesting reference to Resolution 31:

> You have changed the word "servant" to "employee." I would have argued that. Because I insist I stand here as your humble servant; and think well of the virtue of humility. If that is implied in the word "servant," I would have left it in "Public Servants Week." But you have changed that; that's all right. But we stand here as the humble servants of this organization. We want to work to your best advantage. We are handicapped for the necessary resources to equip ourselves, our offices, so that we can do more of the things that ought to be done.

The union delegates left Long Beach with a number of emotions, some of them conflicting. They had witnessed heated debate over (1) a move to share in top level responsibility; (2) the special arrangements, which many members suspected were a means of control from the top; (3) the question of international union representatives coming to conventions with votes other than those of the local or council that sent them; and (4) election of vice-presidents regionally as a way to increase democracy in the union.

Most delegates would have little time to reflect on the international's lofty matters once they got back to their daily concerns. But the impression had been made at the Long Beach convention that all was not so peaceful at the top. Zander had used the words "bile" and "venom." They were probably too strong, too exaggerated, but if the delegates forgot the words themselves, they probably remembered the tone they created.

Wurf: Here Come the Young Turks

The '58 convention signaled the fact the union was changing. Voices were being raised about the direction of the union and the heavyhandedness of the international staff, Zander's staff, led by one Jerry Wurf. Zander won, but he didn't understand the significance of '58 which was that the union was no longer Arnold's little private club.

Zander had the votes in '58, but he was only up against a small, noisy opposition of non-professional rank and filers who were not necessarily liberals as much as they were just people who were annoyed, irritated and distressed. The real significance of 1958 is that it was a prelude to 1960.

It was between the 1958 and 1960 conventions that I left the international staff to become executive director of District Council 37. Zander was becoming less and less a hero to me, and my departure marks the breakdown in our relationship.

I didn't lead the rebellion against Zander. It was started by other guys, and I played honest broker, because both sides could trust me. I didn't think the union could stand the struggle.

A number of younger men were coming into the union, and they were restless. Although the union is a free society, differences are generally resolved by people leaving, rather than by internal confrontations that sharpen differences of opinion. So in a strange way the democratic checks and balances withered as the union grew, and this lack of democratic dynamics was beginning to make a lasting impression.

61

The other development was Zander's disengagement from the central role of the union—to improve the wages, hours and working conditions of is members. His main interests were international affairs—in which, it turned out, he was getting deeply involved with the CIA—and the housing programs—through which he was surrounded by hustlers, thieves and a whole bevy of strange characters.

Even back in 1948 I was appalled at the low caliber of our staff and concerned with the union's lack of success. But because I liked Zander, I did what is common for one who admires an older man: I found rationalizations. I attributed the organization's shortcomings to a bunch of inept people who surrounded Arnold. I was never willing to blame him.

Something else was happening in the '50s. Guys like Joe Ames, Al Bilik, Vic Gotbaum, Norm Schut and Bob Hastings were coming along. They weren't as enchanted as I by the old man, and they were an aggressive, ambitious bunch.

Arnold Zander forgot neither the words nor the tone of his remarks at the 1958 convention. In the October 1958 issue of the union's international newspaper, *The Public Employee*, Zander's signed editorial was entitled "We Need Self-Discipline."

In assessing the needs of our international union recently, we were struck by the lack of discipline in some areas of our organization.

Now the word *discipline* has unfortunate meanings for some, so we shall first attempt to define our precise meaning here. We are referring to the discipline of an organization whose members understand the program decided upon and hew to the line to achieve it. This is not discipline by submission, but discipline imposed by knowledge of goals sought and recognition that an undisciplined organization will flounder and fail.

62

Jerry Wurf (right) in 1950 with Zander, Joseph Keenan and John
DeLury at a dinner honoring DeLury

Self-discipline brings order rather than confusion. Lack of it breeds anarchy. We go to school to discipline our minds to sort out the wheat from the chaff, to learn to make right decisions rather than wrong ones. And an organization needs self-discipline just as an individual does.

. . . Disagreement in a union is healthy. But the disagreements must be aired before the representatives of all the membership—at an international convention. Following the expression of all points of view comes the vote and the decision of the majority. No matter how violently the minority may disagree with the actions of the majority, it is bound by democratic principles to abide by them. Time and again your general officers have disagreed with actions taken by our international conventions. But since they were the expression of the wishes of the majority of the delegates we have abided by them.

It is our contention that a local union or a council can do no less.

Following the decision of the majority is not, in any sense, an indication of being cowed. On the contrary, it shows the courage of abiding by a group decision (which, of course, is more adult than saying that if the game can't be played my way I'll pick up my toys and leave).

Only when there is not the machinery for an orderly review of problems that arise (in our case the International Executive Board and International conventions) is there a possible excuse for mavericks in a trade union. We have that machinery readily available for any disgruntled local or council, so there is no excuse for undisciplined disgression . . . .

On the surface there are few flaws in Zander's logic, but union officials, veterans of convention maneuvering, claim that the method of choosing executive board candidates that lay behind this logic guaranteed a compliant board. One of them, presently an AFSCME international official, explained how the system worked in those pre-Wurf days: "After the nominations had been made from the floor, and on the night before the voting, the administration would go over the list and decide what the slate would be. The favored individuals would then get a knock on their door at midnight, and one of Zander's people would tell them they'd been tapped for the board. The next morning . . . the word would get around the convention as to what the slate was. Rarely did a 'non-tapped' candidate make office."

The method of selection resulted in a board with the same outlook as the international president, and not until the early '60s did it begin to give the administration any real opposition to its pet projects. This situation, plus the fact that the board met only two or three times a year, kept control of the union squarely in the hands of international headquarters and Zander. The closeness between the executive board and the administration began to bother those locals and councils that felt the board should play a checks and balances role. This feeling would grow as opposition to Zander increased after the 1958 convention.

Wurf's mistrust of the way Zander was running the union was confirmed by the news that shortly after the '58 convention the president was planning a three month tour of Africa. Wurf was shocked, and he told Zander it was no time to go abroad when internal affairs needed attention, when there were so many fences to be mended. Zander disagreed and told Wurf he felt the Washington staff could handle things in his absence.

Wurf: A Strained Relationship

I was still one of Arnold's boys, but the relationship was strained and my tolerance was wearing thin. I was in Washington for some reason, and Zander announced he was off for

Africa for several months, even though the union was in trouble. He asked if I wanted to go with him, which was idiotic. I told him it was wrong to go; he said I'd convinced him, but he was going anyway.

Zander changed the subject. He said he wanted a black official of the union to go to Africa with him. I recommended James Farmer, later the civil rights leader who directed freedom rides in Alabama and Mississippi. Farmer was a Council 37 organizer at the time.

While they were gone, Chapman ran headquarters, and it was chaos—the whole national union was a total mess. So I came into headquarters, and by this time Leo Kramer was powerfully entrenched, and we got into a big discussion. I must admit it was significant that for the first time Kramer was talking to me as a peer. Chapman was very upset by my complaints. He didn't understand that my real beef was that the union was being badly run. He was not exercising real administrative authority. In reality he was caught up in a foot race with Kramer over who was in charge during Zander's absence. Chapman wasn't secure enough, and he didn't have the staff support to cope with administering the union. Kramer, on the other hand, was anxious to prove his ability, but he simply wasn't succeeding. The fact is, sound administration simply wasn't possible in that environment of competition and distrust.

Ames, Blatz, Schut, Bilik—some of the men who were emerging as leaders at the 1958 convention—were unlike Wurf in that they were not so closely tied to Zander, so it is ironic that Wurf would become their leader. No matter how great the discontent, without power change is impossible. Zander was old, entrenched, polite, but dogmatic and immune to criticism. Wurf was young, on the make, ready and powerful.

But for the moment Wurf was still in Zander's camp.

Wurf: *You must remember, in those days I was Arnold Zander's hatchet man. I had some questions as to what he should have been doing, but I saw my function as helping Arnold to bring the union around to the principles of active trade unionism. I had to do a lot of things that really didn't make me the most popular guy. But I did them because I believed in Zander.*

It is surprising that Wurf's opposition to the Africa trip did not make a greater impression on Zander. Wurf's record of service to the union was impeccable: he was an able organizer and bargainer, he was loyal at a time of dissension in the ranks. Had Zander not felt so firmly in control of the situation, he might have listened when his "fair-haired boy" spoke up. Instead Zander invited special attention to the trip by devoting two editorials in *The Public Employee* to the importance of helping "the struggling public employee unions of the young African nations."

In 1959 Wurf had been with the union for eleven years, and in that time he had risen to prominence as a regional director, an international staff man who ran New York City's Council 37. He was responsible for building 37 into the union's single most powerful council, a goal achieved in 1958 by the signing of Executive Order 49 by Mayor Robert Wagner. The order established limited collective bargaining rights for unions that represented a majority of employees in any given city department, and in Wurf's view it ultimately led to President Kennedy's Executive Order 10998 granting federal employees the rights of workers in private industry unions.

Union newspaper headlines in 1959 reflect Wurf's success:

- N.Y. Council 37 Certified as Executive Bargaining Agent for Two Departments (February)
- New York Bridge and Tunnel Authority Signs Contract Covering 600 Employees (March)

67

- N.Y. Council 37 Gets City to End Stall on Negotiations (May)
- N.Y. Council 37 Sets Sights on Clerical-Administrative Employees (November)
- N.Y. Council 37 Institutes Program to Strengthen Bargaining (December)

In April 1959 there were indications that Wurf's hair was turning not so fair and that Zander was becoming even more aloof from the membership. The strongest sign was the appointment of Leo Kramer as administrative assistant in charge of all membership matters. Kramer, who had joined the union three years after Wurf, had gained a position of power and authority, and unlike Wurf, his temperament suited Zander.

Late in 1959 Wurf resigned from the international staff to become executive director of Council 37. It is not clear whether Zander regretted Wurf's departure or if he could anticipate that his former loyal follower would become a persistent nemesis. Zander claims he made no move to dissuade Wurf from leaving, Wurf insists he did, and the disagreement is indicative of a falling out still to come.

Zander was preoccupied with the housing program. In June *The Public Employee* carried a story of the ground breaking ceremony for the Zander Apartments in Milwaukee, the first of a series of union housing projects. Martin K. Frank, a real estate developer, had become the union's consultant in a program to build a series of low cost apartment complexes with federally guaranteed loans.

It was never clear to the membership what AFSCME's role was in the financing and construction of the projects, and for that reason the housing program would become an internal political issue as opposition to Zander gained momentum.

It was also late in 1959—in October—that the incipient opposition forces held a meeting in Columbus, Ohio. "It was called by Bob Hastings and Al Bilik," Ames remembers, "and attended by about a dozen of us, including Wurf. It was devoted wholly to a discussion of union policies and structure and our concerns, and immediately afterward Wurf went to Washington and reported on the meeting to Zander, as had been agreed to beforehand."

There was yet another meeting, in Chicago in early 1960, a few months before that year's convention in Philadelphia. Although on Zander's staff, Wurf recalls his role as that of mediator or "honest broker," and says now he was by then cooler to Zander than anyone suspected.

To Wurf the significance of the Chicago meeting was not so much what was decided as who was there—not the group that "kicked up a fuss at Long Beach but a different group, college guys with an intellectual background."

Says Ames: "The Chicago meeting was a chance for our thinking to jell a little more. A report on the meeting was made by Wurf to Zander, with the full consent and knowledge of the rest of us."

The Philadelphia convention opened on April 25, 1960, and the membership was in an apprehensive mood. Since Long Beach the issues had not died down; they had crystallized.

As the convention began, Wurf was still loyal to Zander to the extent that he saw himself as an intermediary between the administration and the dissidents, the one man open to hearing complaints who was still trusted enough to present them to Zander. Ames, Bilik, Gotbaum, Hastings and Schut had told Wurf in Chicago what problems they saw within the union, and though Wurf did not agree with them totally, he promised to try to arrange a meeting with Zander.

The dissidents came to the convention ready to bargain with Zander: if he would grant a number of reforms to democratize the union, they would cooperate and use their considerable floor muscle in support of what he wanted more than anything else from the 1960 convention: a per capita tax increase to one dollar, a raise of thirty-five cents per member.

There was no disagreement, as Joe Ames points out, that

69

the union was underfinanced. Many newer locals were already paying a dollar, so it would have been only fair to raise the per capita across the board. The disagreement was over what was being done with the money.

By 1960 several more housing projects were underway, and although most members considered them a noble under-taking, they were disturbed by the vague way the projects had been described and the misleading answers they received when they tried to get more information. The membership was being assured that the projects were cost-free and without financial liability. In truth, under FHA regulations the union was "sponsoring" the project, meaning it was lending its name as a nonprofit organization to certain builders and con-tractors in order for them to get government loans at special, below average interest rates. The theory was that such an arrangement would allow public housing to be built cheaply enough to stimulate the interest of commercial contractors. As the sponsor, AFSCME did become liable for certain amounts, both of building expenses and government financ-ing. Suspecting something of the sort, Ames and his group were trying to determine and make known to the membership the nature and amount of that liability.

Another point that bothered the dissidents was the fre-quency and duration of Zander's overseas trips and emphasis on international affairs.

Wurf made good on his promise to the dissidents to pre-sent their case, and on the day before the convention opened, after informal agreement had been reached with Zander, Wurf and Schut met in a hotel room with Kramer and Tom Morgan, the director of organization, to negotiate reforms. After several hours an agreement was reached: the reformists would support the dollar per capita tax increase and the ad-ministration would not oppose regional election of vice-presi-dents. According to Wurf they even agreed on a districting formula for the election of vice-presidents.

But the satisfaction of compromise was ephemeral, as the

70

word was out on Monday morning that the administration had changed its mind. "Whatever the reason," Ames recalls, "we'd been double-crossed."

The opposition leaders, with Wurf now committed to them, confronted Zander and Kramer at a meeting of the laws committee and demanded to know if it were true there was to be no compromise. The argument centered on the districting formula, whereupon Kramer denied there had ever been a deal.

As Wurf recalls it today, "I put Tom Morgan in a hell of a spot. I turned to all the people there and said, 'Now I know Tom Morgan is an honest man. Let's ask him. Tom, did we or did we not come to an agreement last night?' "

Morgan was a Zander appointee, and his job was on the line, but he said, "We came to an agreement," and pointing to a map delineating the districts, he said further, "and that's what we agreed to."

The entire New York delegation—Councils 37 and 50, the upstate council of which Al Wurf, Jerry's brother, was an official—had voted to support the per capita tax increase. When he was convinced of the double-cross, Jerry Wurf decided to call an early (Tuesday) morning caucus and reverse the decision, even if it meant splitting up the New York delegation.

Wurf called his brother and asked him to come to the meeting, and Al, a Zander man, insisted that a face to face meeting with the president would resolve the disagreements.

A meeting did occur, though there are different accounts of what took place and its importance. Kramer gave his interpretation in *Labor's Paradox:*

Attempts at Compromise
In the middle of the night on Monday, the president was awakened and asked to come to a meeting of the opposition. At this meeting he continued to ignore personal attacks, but he heard references to

disaffiliation and to joining other unions that had opposed the federation for years. The report of the next morning's board meeting gives a quiet summary, in contrast with the realities of that bizarre night:

President Zander reviewed Amendments #35 and #36, mentioning that he had spoken to the laws committee the previous night when they met. He also spoke about the amendment establishing a budget stating that he had told the committee that if the board wanted it, they could request it, but it didn't necessarily have to be a constitutional amendment. President Zander apprised the board members of meetings he had had with Jerry Wurf, Al Bilik, Bob Hastings, and others, regarding these controversial amendments. In regard to the election of vice presidents by regions, he mentioned that several maps had been worked on dividing the regions both by our staff and by those who had submitted the amendment. President Zander also stated that the opposition felt strongly about the budget idea and also the quarterly meetings of the international executive board, but he felt sure there could be a compromise. He also believed there could be a compromise on the regional setup as there are advantages to election in such manner. He suggested the board work on it in the afternoon when not in session to see if harmony could be attained.

Ames, calling the meeting "the most significant in the internal politics of the union," gives this account:

Zander joined us in Jerry's suite at about 2 a.m. It was an unpleasant meeting, but the last thing on our minds was to quit the union. Arnold did agree that the matter of regionalism would be taken up before the per capita tax vote and that he would not

72

oppose our proposal, but he indicated his own staff might oppose it.

Every present and former follower of Wurf who figured in the Philadelphia meeting disputes Kramer's version of what happened. Zander says that he has no clear recollection of either meeting as being of particular significance.

Whatever the case, one thing is clear and historically documented: the 1960 convention swiftly deteriorated into a near brawl. On the floor shouting and recrimination became frequent, almost common. Speakers were purposely delayed by a variety of techniques including the lengthy roll call procedure; name-calling was frequent and acrimonious; and the chair wielded the gavel with a decidedly heavy hand. Off the floor it was more of the same, but that was expected; what wasn't expected was the atmosphere of what Ames has termed "open warfare."

Zander's refusal to compromise with the dissidents pushed them over the brink. For several years Wurf had been vacillating, realizing that his support of Zander was based on past loyalties, past positions. What occurred was the end of a lengthy transformation that he described as "a whole gradual erosion of confidence in Zander institutionally and personally."

Wurf: "Now You Lead Us Out"

Norm Schut and I were having breakfast on Sunday, the day before the convention was to open in Philadelphia. Lola Zander called over from a nearby table with a suggestion that we go down and talk to Arnold. I was embarrassed and said something to the effect that it wasn't so easy to communicate with Arnold any more, since everything had to be cleared through five people.

She persisted, saying, "I want you boys to go see him," and though I felt a little old to be called a "boy," I said we would.

73

Norm and I spent an hour or two with Arnold without Kramer or anybody else there, and we reached an agreement on what Arnold would support, in exchange for which we agreed to try to persuade the guys to support Arnold on the per capita thing. There had been a good bit of give by the insurgents, so I figured they could feel they took a little back on the regionalism compromise.

I remember meeting then with the guys and was sort of their hero. Everybody was delighted because nobody really wanted a big beef with the old man.

On opening day we didn't like the rumors of no compromise or what Zander had to say to the convention, but we didn't take any of it too seriously. Then on Monday night the laws committee met. Schut and I were both on that committee, which is where the big stuff was to take place. Arnold came in, and he proceeded to turn around on every single agreement we had reached the day before.

I couldn't believe my ears. Schut turned to Zander, and Schut is not like I am, given to bad language. He doesn't often lose his temper either; he's a very cool cookie, and he said to Zander, "You bastard. You double-crossed us."

Later we learned that Kramer, realizing that if the reforms went through he wouldn't be able to dominate the union, talked Arnold out of them. And Arnold, as is so often the way with true blue intellecturals, had no trouble gainsaying on Monday what he had agreed to on Sunday.

So I went back to a meeting with the insurgents and reported what had happened. All hell broke loose, and Ames made a statement I will never forget: "You led us into this, Jerry. Now you lead us out."

The official proceedings barely reflect the bizarre activities and angry emotions of that convention, but they are easy to spot between the lines.

As the days progressed, the dissidents, burned by their failure, resorted to obstructionism and truculence. Zander was able to control who spoke by recognizing or ignoring a delegate, many of whom became increasingly angry at what they felt was calculated oversight.

When regionalism was debated, a Connecticut delegate said bluntly, "I believe in the regional set-up. I don't think this particular thing goes quite far enough, but it is a step in the right direction, and the only time you are going to have a complete, a good organization is when your regional directors are also elected by your people within the regions. We know in New England what it is to have regional directors shoved down our throats. We know what Leo Kramer did in New England . . ."

At one point so many roll call votes had been requested that Wurf rose to request that a roll call vote *not* be asked for: ". . . this convention will not move if we go through a roll call. Even if it means the defeat of this amendment, I urge those of us who support this motion not to request a roll call, so that this convention can proceed to take up some more business." Ames never let Wurf forget that one more roll call might have made the difference at that convention.

By Friday the mood of opposition had reached the edge of rebellion. In an emotional outburst Wurf rose and shouted:

> Mr. Chairman, I think you are making an appeal not for democracy, not to preserve the rights of the small locals, but an appeal to make it impossible for unions that want to weld together, to grow, to get proper representation in this convention. I am tempted to bring a request for a roll call vote. I will leave that to some other delegate. But I think the chair is treating the large locals shabbily. The vote was for us the first time. You used a demagogic appeal. I don't know what has happened to you. It is not becoming of you President Zander.

By the time the smoke had cleared, the regionalism motion had been defeated, but so had a request for a salary increase for Zander and the secretary-treasurer and so had the per capita tax increase.

The transcript of the proceedings has been carefully edited, but one does not have to read between the lines to understand the mood of the convention on the last day. McEntee described an obviously doomed motion:

> It looks like it is the decision to put it on the table or put it on ice or put it wherever you want to put it. Maybe we ought to table the International—and I guess there are a lot of tables back where we go too.
>
> I guess it is time that the chairman got out of order, because pretty nearly everybody has been out of order since we came here.

Wurf: The Meaning of Philadelphia

It was a useless, meaningless convention, full of acrimony, but there wasn't even a hint that this was the beginning of a leadership split. The effort at the convention was not to beat Zander but to democratize the union.

There were several roll call votes—on voting rights, election of officers, autonomy of local affiliates, for example—but Arnold would't give an inch. In turn, he couldn't get his per capita tax. It was a standoff.

Zander's childish response after the convention was to write in an editorial in the union paper that he had survived an "onslaught by the forces of evil." For a while after that we referred to ourselves as FOE.

Even worse, there were attempts to punish the leaders of the opposition: to take over their unions, knock them out of the box with illegal trusteeships and so on. They took some swipes at Council 37, but we were a strong union and could kick back hard, so they stopped swinging.

Kramer came to visit me over a weekend. I had this cottage in Harriman, N.Y., which I bought just before Mildred and I got married. Kramer wanted to talk about get-

76

ting together with Arnold. I said sure, but I insisted he meet not just with me but with our Council 37 executive board.

Kramer tried to soften me up before the meeting by saying, "Name 10 issues, Jerry, and how many would we disagree on—one or two, maybe." It was the kind of bunk that I, as an old demagogue, could recognize.

Arnold came to our board meeting, and some of our people were itchy because of his indecency at the convention but particularly his subsequent attempt to buy up some of our people and turn them against us. Instead of saying let's put the past behind us, Arnold opened the meeting by offering to forgive us for the dreadful things we had done.

I remember spunky Fannie Fine, as astonished as the rest of us, sputtering back at Zander, "What do you mean, forgive us? For what? For not letting you run this union like Hitler?"

Bill McEntee of Philadelphia had arranged for me to meet with Zander later at a restaurant. I told Zander: "Arnold, even if you're right—which your're not—you don't treat people like that. You don't behave that way in front of people who have committed themselves, worked their ass off for this union. They don't think they're evil. On the contrary, they think you are less than decent. But whoever is right or wrong, you have managed to rekindle their hostility."

When I was through, it was clear Zander had no comprehension of what had happened in Philadelphia.

At the Philadelphia Convention in 1960. International staff member Wurf at a committee meeting (above); Zander and Chapman (below) after their reelection without opposition

5.   Milwaukee: Victory in Defeat

During the hectic 1960 convention, feeling betrayed on the regionalism issue, Ames, Hastings, Bilik, Gotbaum and Schut met with Wurf to discuss their next move. They were the group that had met in Chicago to discuss what they felt was the erosion of democracy within the union. Wurf had attended the earlier meeting as a Zander man, but by the end of the 1960 convention Wurf, completely disenchanted with Zander, not only agreed with the anti-Zander forces, he was ready to lead them.

The opposition was not well-organized; it even had difficulty deciding on its name. Forces of Evil (FOE) was discarded for obvious reasons, but there wasn't unanimous consent for the one that was picked. At a meeting in Columbus, Ohio, the dissidents officially formed the Committee on Union Responsibility (COUR). As with most acronyms there were advantages and disadvantages. COUR supporters pronounced it "core," playing on identification with the respected civil rights organization, the Congress on Racial Equality (CORE). COUR detractors pronounced it "cower," and to this day Ames wishes his recommendation had carried—to call it the Committee on Union Problems (COUP).

In the early months of 1961 COUR had no idea of its own constituency and about as much knowledge of its strength. It was started by people like Ames, Bilik, Hastings, Gotbaum and Schut, dissidents who shared frustration over ballot counting procedures that for years had kept power in the grasp of small city or rural locals and councils that Zander controlled.

Wurf: *The mucilage that held us together was our desire to democratize the union, whether we came from a small local in Connecticut or a large council in New York City. We were outraged at the way the union was being administered, and the weaknesses of its constitutional structure became even more apparent when a heavyhanded guy like Kramer became a force because of the dilettante way Zander ran things.*

It wasn't an ideological thing. Some of us were liberals; some of us were not. You could say we were all labor intellectuals; we were savvy, we had strong ideas. With the exception of Schut who's a political scientist, we were well-grounded trade unionists.

To a man the dissidents also shared a resentment over the way local union affairs were being run by international staffers under trusteeships and other special arrangements.

Wurf: *Special arrangements were originally conceived to make professional resources of the national union available to locals for legislative or organizational campaigns or what have you. What Zander did was distort the concept of special arrangements by using them to take over the policy-making mechanism of the locals and councils. It was another example of authoritarian administraton.*

The founders of COUR believed that even though the housing programs, Zander's trips abroad and his involvement in Public Services International (an international scretariat of public service unions) were humanitarian efforts, they were misdirected and drained the resources of leadership at a time when the union faced serious internal problems. As Hastings recalls, "The union was turning into a goddamn housing corporation and a second State Department."

There was a marked difference between the public statements of Arnold Zander and Jerry Wurf at this time, a difference that cannot be easily passed off as a traditional ins versus

80

outs confrontation. Their philosophical gap was widening.

"Labor News Conference," the AFL-CIO's Mutual Network radio program, featured Arnold Zander as its guest November 20, 1961. The questioners were John Herling of the National Newspaper Syndicate and Alex Uhl, editor at Press Associates, Inc. Herling's first question had to do with AFSCME's being "one of the growth unions of the American labor movement."

ZANDER: Well, Mr. Herling, our union has a tremendous popularity. We should have 1,500,000 to 2,000,000 members in state-local government service. We now have 220,000 so you see we have a long way to go. Everything being equal, we should be growing rapidly within the next year. . . . We have more than doubled in the last ten years. We've added more than 20,000 last year and so we anticipate getting the next 50,000 quite rapidly. . . .

UHL: Do you think. . . Mr. Zander, that the "white collar" worker. . . is beginning to realize that he must have organization if he's to maintain a standard of living that is adequate?

ZANDER: I think this understanding is growing, Mr. Uhl, and our growth is to a considerable extent in the "white collar" area. I think this will go on. We are getting more professionals in our union all the time. We have a large female membership. We have a very large Negro membership. I mention that in passing because it is not thought of in connection with the public service. But we are getting more and more "white collar" workers, professional workers; I think our growth possibilities are increasing in those areas.

HERLING: Mr. Zander, aren't you the International President of an AFL-CIO affiliate who's a Ph.D., a Doctor of Philosophy?

ZANDER: That's right. I earned it the hard way. I got a Ph.D. in Public Administration from the University of Wisconsin many years ago, and I'm happy to have it because I needed the additional education which some people don't need.

UHL: Well then, do you feel as a "white collar" person par excellence, your dignity, your character in the community has been belittled by your association with the trade movement?

ZANDER: No, I have been proud of my work all through these years, and am sure will continue to be. I think our work has made a very substantial contribution to the democratic processes in state and local government and for the high level of performance. We are very proud of the effect our union has had, and the kind of service the public is getting. . . .

HERLING: Actually the Wisconsin idea with which you were associated from the very start actually is an example of the state as a social laboratory, is it not?

ZANDER: That is correct. We took the view there in our work that only the best should serve the state, and the state should serve responsibly all the people of the community and it should be integrated into the state community under the state commonwealth. The state service should be administered by professionals, by technicians, and not by people placed there for partisan reasons. . . .

HENRY W. FLANNERY (moderator): What percentage of the potential membership do you have now? What is your goal per se the next year?

ZANDER: Well, as I said, we should have a million and a half. We have 220,000. We're below 15 per cent. We're expecting a growth of some 50,000 in the next year. I think that's a reasonable potential

82

growth for us. Driven by our coming convention and some hard work, we'll get that much growth.

HERLING: The type of personnel you have in the country, your organizing personnel, are they pretty high level? That's one of the problems I think in any big growth organization.

ZANDER: Yes, we do have. We have a good staff. We have a structure different from some. We employ counsels at the state level much more than others because we deal with 50 sovereign governments you see in our federal system here, so that we have had to develop strong mechanisms at the state level, and we have those functioning very well. . . .

Two weeks later Wurf was on the hustings, clearly a candidate. He spoke to an AFSCME audience in Concord, California. The sharp tone and angry substance cannot all be attributed to campaign rhetoric. He explained his outbursts in Philadelphia by reciting COUR's complaints about Zander's administration—the compliant executive board, special arrangements, centralization of power, housing and international programs. Then he summarized his platform:

I could go on and on and on telling you that in effect we have a union which is failing because it no longer has confidence in the only real asset it has. I can tell you if you read the last financial report you will see that we lost a tremendous sum of money in the last quarter; you will see that we spent a sum in expenses equal, almost equal, to the amount of money we spent in wages. You will find that there is more energy and activity spent on the Zander Apartments in Los Angeles, the Zander Apartments in Milwaukee, the contemplated Zander Apartments in St. Paul, and so on and so forth, than there is in building this union.

83

You will find that the whole theory, the whole concept that brought this union into business—believe it or not the concept that brought Arnold Zander into the great union movement—has been completely abandoned, that Zander now has to compromise with the very people whom he has always said he detested in the union.

Again, I'm taking much longer than I intended and that happens to the kind of people who have the brazenness to stand up and speak without notes.

I want to say this in conclusion. We started this campaign, we put a guy forward as a candidate—myself—now Gordon Chapman is a candidate for Secretary-Treasurer, and I suspect—I know, I don't suspect, I know—that when my name was first put forward it was merely a vehicle for communication to dramatize our concern with what's wrong in the International Union because we didn't really know what was going on all over the country.

As the time went on, as these meetings took place, as Arnold and I met and other people met with Arnold, as people heard Arnold or as people began to take their grievances and write us about it, something very interesting happened. It became apparent that our candidacies were meaningful, that we had a more than fair chance of winning.

These excerpts reflect the positions and the postures of the two candidates as they headed for the 1962 convention in Milwaukee. Zander was running on his record, and Wurf was using that record against him.

Wurf: *I had a great little secretary in those days, but she was always getting appointments screwed up, and I didn't have the guts to fire her. On that trip to California, where I was to debate Zander, she messed up my schedule, causing me*

84

to miss my plane to Los Angeles. The flight I missed crashed in Jamaica Bay. I got the next one to L.A., still pretty shaken up, and flew by helicopter to Riverside. And right after I got out of the helicopter—I was only four steps from it—a gust of wind or something caught the chopper, and it keeled over barely missing me. Needless to say I was in pretty poor shape for the debate.

The major issue of the COUR program was democratic reform, which specifically called for:

- regionalism
- return of effective power to the office of secretary-treasurer
- more authority for the executive board
- voting reform
- decentralization of power and an end to special arrangements.

Yet perhaps more appealing to the electorate were the subsidiary issues of fiscal irresponsibility and possible corruption (the housing program) and inattention to internal union problems (Zander's preoccupation with international matters and his many trips abroad).

The housing program had come about almost by accident. In the late 1950s Zander was getting complaints that the growing international staff did not have enough parking spaces at union headquarters in Washington. He contacted the owners of some adjacent property and as a result came to know and greatly admire Martin K. Frank. Frank was a real estate developer, builder and promoter. Later, because of his handling of the housing projects he came to be called a crook by the COUR faction, though Zander insists to this day on his absolute honesty. Frank brokered the deal between the federal government and the union whereby, under a special provision of the Federal Housing Act, the union acted as nonprofit sponsor for the construction of multifamily housing units for people displaced by urban renewal projects.

Construction of the first apartments was begun in

85

Milwaukee, April 24, 1959. By December 1960 ground had been broken for apartments in Puerto Rico; their purpose was to promote the union's organizational drive in the Commonwealth, although Tom Morgan inspected the project and reported, "I wouldn't let my dog live there." There was an AFSCME housing project started in downtown Los Angeles in 1961, and on March 9, 1962 *The Public Employee* carried an announcement of one to be built in Cambridge, Massachusetts. A fifth project planned for St. Paul, Minnesota was abandoned.

The rank and file was let in on few of the details of the housing program, but Wurf was asked about it in Concord, California. His response:

> There has been a lot of activity, a lot of effort and a lot of time by the International Union in what has been called a series of housing projects; a set of apartments was built in Milwaukee, Wisconsin and they are called the Zander Apartments. There is presently being built what I am told are a set of apartments in the Los Angeles area. . . called the Zander Apartments.
>
> The people in St. Paul looked up one day and read the union newspaper and found that the Central Body had been trying to get the city to go along with them on some kind of housing project in St. Paul, and a man appeared before the City Board that handled these matters and said on behalf of the International Union, on behalf of President Zander he was bidding for the land that the Central Body had originally intended for a project sponsored by the Central Body there and there was much resentment by the Central Body and by our local unions in St. Paul who knew nothing about this and still don't, although there seems to be some continued activity.

The criticism of the situation or the point I was trying to make—and in this effort to say so much in such a little time I may have perhaps confused matters and I want to set the record straight—that Arnold, when he has spoken about this thing has talked about the fact that in 20 or 30 or 40 years, it's not important how long, the union in return for the effort and whatever money may or may not go into it at this time, will have a legacy. I think that is the exact word he used in terms of the investment we put into these apartments and time and effort, and the government puts a 100 per cent or 90 per cent mortgage—I'm not sure of the exact details—and many of us have criticized this activity on this ground, that it has taken considerable time and effort and so on to build these apartment houses. They are not built in terms of any special, particular social need, that if there is a particular and special social need, we would suspect that there are many other community resources better qualified to handle this than this International Union, and so we would hope that the legacy of this union is a couple of million members and a collective bargaining agreement in every jurisdiction across the country. . . .

Wurf's charge that the housing projects were not undertaken "for any special, particular social need" deeply hurt Zander, who regarded the program a fitting monument to his 25 years' stewardship. Tom Morgan, who was fired in 1960 and was no partisan of Zander's thereafter, expressed the opinion of many other old-time officials of the union: "He saw the housing projects as his monument; instead, it turned out to be an albatross around his neck. He should have known that the only real monument for a labor leader is the members."

The housing program would not become an albatross until later, but in the months prior to the 1962 convention it was clear that COUR was successful in its effort to make the membership ask if housing was a valid union enterprise.

As for the foreign trips, it was not easy for the rank and file to understand how an African or Asian trip by their president was hurting the union at home. Nevertheless the COUR forces continued to press their case that Zander was guilty of absentee management.

As the 1962 convention approached, Wurf had no clear idea of his chances. He had had no way to gauge the effect he was having on the rank and file. What he lacked most obviously was a forum, and the incumbent administration made the most of that disadvantage. As is the case in any large union, the administration controlled the two main routes of access to the rank and file: the official union publication and the mailing list of members.

The first route was closed to COUR, and Zander quite naturally pressed his advantage by careful use of editorial and news space on behalf of his position, and as an entrenched official he was able to employ the tactic of pretending the opposition did not exist. When the executive board met in April and voted to reject the regionalism plan, the decision was featured in a three and one-half page article in the April issue of *The Public Employee*. The article contained a reprint of a report on regionalism done for the union by Harvard Professor John T. Dunlop, a recognized labor expert. Dunlop concluded: "There is no objective basis for the view that either system of selecting executive board members is more or less democratic than the other. The crucial test is the impact of any constitutional change upon the capacity of the international union to grow in the decade ahead. The proposal for election of international executive board members by districts is unlikely to increase the capacity to organize and it might well adversely retard the rate of growth." The Dunlop statement still infuriates Wurf, who calls it "bizarre" and "absurd."

Wurf got little mention in *The Public Employee,* but beginning in mid-1961 stories about his brother Al appeared frequently. Al, who remained a Zander loyalist through the 1962 campaign, was named the union's director for New York state in early 1961.

The other main power of the incumbent, control over the mailing list, became an early issue between COUR and Zander forces. After frequent requests, denied on the basis that only duly elected officers had the right to use membership lists, the dissidents could only retaliate by stressing their disadvantage whenever any of them addressed an AFSCME gathering. Actually some bootleg lists did get into the hands of Wurf forces, slipped to them by friendly staff personnel at headquarters. They were therefore able to send their newsletter, but there was no way they could assess its effect. That was their main problem.

Recognizing the need to focus and formalize its efforts, COUR held its first formal meeting in Milwaukee in early 1961 and met about two months later in Columbus, Ohio to nominate Wurf for president. Bob Hastings was elected secretary of COUR, and Charles Oldham, Ames' administrative assistant in Local 410, St. Louis, was named treasurer.

On May 15, 1961 Secretary-Treasurer Chapman was appointed by President Kennedy to a post in the State Department. *The Public Employee* announced the appointment in glowing terms:

> After more than 24 years of devoted service to our International Union, Secretary-Treasurer Gordon W. Chapman has submitted his resignation, effective May 15, 1961, to accept an appointment as special assistant to the Secretary of State.
>
> In his new post Brother Chapman will serve as Coordinator of International Labor Affairs, one of the top assignments in the State Department. In

this capacity he will work with the U.S. Department of Labor, with international labor organizations, on overseas labor coordination, and on compilation of international labor statistics.

On July 26 in an open letter to the membership Zander announced his intention of doing away with the elective position of international secretary-treasurer. The move abetted the COUR cause, for it demonstrated Zander's tendency to take authoritarian, unilateral action. This was also the effect—although in a less significant way—of Zander's decision to impose a trusteeship on Wurf-leaning Council 55 in Lansing, Michigan.

Wurf: *Zander's getting rid of Chapman and trying to get the executive board not to fill the position—his hangup being there should be only one officer at headquarters—was a powerful dynamic in our fight against the old man. You've got to understand first of all that people were appalled by the heavyhandedness of the 1958 and 1960 conventions. Number two, Chapman, although a man without strong convictions, was amiable and well-liked.*

A lot of people who had no desire to take on Zander or get involved in the other issues were really distressed by the Chapman departure, and the fight to retain a secretary-treasurer was a very powerful issue.

Zander reiterated his position on the secretary-treasurer issue in *The Public Employee* on October 30:

President Arnold S. Zander has announced he will recommend to the 1962 AFSCME convention that the office of secretary-treasurer be made a post that deals exclusively with fiscal matters.

"There has been considerable interest expressed throughout our organization concerning my attitude toward the secretary-treasurer's job," Zander said.

"It is my deep personal conviction that the

90

Delegates demonstrate for Zander-Lima ticket at the 1962 convention in Milwaukee

provision for electing a secretary-treasurer should be changed by the convention and that a comptroller should be appointed to provide all necessary checks and balances on fiscal controls.

"In keeping with our civil service traditions, the comptroller should be selected on the basis of his professional qualifications. He, along with the international executive board, should be given every necessary authority for setting up a system of checks and balances in regard to the finances of our international union. . . ."

"I would like to emphasize," President Zander said, "that I seek no new authorities not already granted me by the present constitution.

"Nor is my suggestion for change new. Years ago, at the very beginning of our international union, I urged that the post of secretary-treasurer not be an elected political post.

"My reasoning then and now is that if the convention elects both the president and the secretary-treasurer, it elects two executive officers who find themselves in dual and frequently confused leadership roles."

Zander said further that the position of secretary-treasurer caused "conflicting political loyalties to spring up in the union" and that this in turn created confusion in the field because of the possibility of conflicting orders from the leadership. He defended himself against the charge of a power play by insisting he had all the authority he could use or need under the constitution. He tried to appeal to his opposition by insisting that when a successor took over he should have a free hand in creating his own administration and not be burdened with a second elective office. Finally he stated that the true function of a secretary-treasurer should be to confine himself exclusively to fiscal matters, rather than play politics, and that he would not do that so long as he was elected rather than appointed.

The final countdown for the 1962 election began in the summer of '61:

- In August the executive board appointed James L. McCormack, the senior member of the AFSCME regional director staff, secretary-treasurer over Zander's objections.
- In September the big Ohio delegation voted to support Wurf.
- In November the convention site was changed from Kansas City to Milwaukee, and the Zander Apartments in Milwaukee were dedicated. (The reason for the site shift, Wurf says, was Zander's determination to convene on his home ground.)
- In March 1962 the executive board endorsed Zander's request for an increase in the per capita tax.
- In April the candidates for secretary-treasurer were announced: Tom Morgan was to be Wurf's running mate; George Lima would run with Zander. Lima, a black, had supported eliminating the post of secretary-treasurer.

Whether or not he knew it in early 1962, Wurf had an audience of members who would be delegates to the convention. They had begun to listen to his charges and were becoming anxious to hear the administration's defense. With no way to gauge the effect they were having on the membership the COURites did not know their own strength; consequently they went into the convention with no hope of winning. The best they hoped for was to force some reforms on the Zander administration. If they had been able to read the signs and played to win, they might have surprised themselves with victory.

In his opening remarks to the delegates at the 1962 convention Zander made an unusual and unfortunate symbolic

93

reference. "The day outdoors isn't too pleasant," he said. "It has its compensations, however. I don't know if all of you recognized the fog horn when it was blowing these last couple of days... I heard it, and although I was unaware of the reason for the sound, the fog horn blowing almost always seemed to occur on a dark day during my youth."

Aside from relating that the convention would get used to the cantankerous public address system, "...just as we become accustomed to a fog horn," Zander made no additional metaphoric use of the opening symbol. But there were many in the auditorium who knew that the main function of a fog horn is to warn of hidden dangers ahead.

If Arnold Zander considered any of the COUR charges as hidden dangers, he gave no indication of it in his long opening address. One by one he ticked off most of the opposition party's main complaints, not by reference to COUR or Wurf, but simply as items to explain to the convention.

For example, Zander was fiercely proud of the housing program and met the criticism of it head on:

> I am aware of the fact that this matter [housing] had been bruited about in recent [years] and I am going to give you the record. . . . we have performed the task of the function of non-profit sponsoring of relocation housing. . . . To do that job we had to do it with our housing chairman, a man whom I regard as absolutely the most competent in this area of anybody so engaged. He has a high degree of competence and he has knowledge in this field, unquestionable capacity, deep devotion. He has carried the brunt of this problem and made it possible to do what we have done.

He went on to explain the costs in Milwaukee and Puerto Rico, stressing that the program had cost the union none of its own money and very little of his time, and then he turned to a specific case that had been the source of several ugly rumors.

94

He explained how the union, following the merger of the AFL-CIO, had come to be involved in organizing in Panama and then how the housing program in Puerto Rico was intimately related to the goal of organizing on the island. He referred to Richard Fincke, the president of a company called Transamerican Industries, who had business experience in both Panama and Puerto Rico.

Because Zander was so interested in developing the union in Puerto Rico and because he believed Fincke to be "a very convincing and able and intelligent 'gentleman'," Zander arranged a $40,000 union loan to Transamerican Industries.

Admitting that Fincke had stopped making payments on the loan, Zander sounded defensive:

> Now, one makes this kind of investment in the light of circumstances at the time. It seemed to our leadership and to our executive board included, that that was at least not an unwise thing to do. If it was an error it was an error with every good intention but now it is being employed as a device for crucifixion.

This divine imagery so unsettled some of the delegates that they began to mutter. Zander ignored the muttering and continued, for he had a surprise for his critics:

> Now, realizing the efforts that have been made to exploit this transaction and the satisfaction which has been gotten from it, I somewhat hesitate to take from these critics the joy they are experiencing in having their morsel to roll around their tongues but, at the same time and in keeping with my efforts this morning to give you some facts, I think you will be interested in knowing that I have here a cashier's check. . . .

Zander is tall, at least six foot three. With his arms fully extended skyward he makes a striking impression. At this

95

point he took the check and held it high above his head. He waved it slowly back and forth in front of the assembled delegates as he spoke:

> . . .not a personal check, a cashier's check in the amount of $12,000 made out to Richard Fincke and endorsed to the Federation by him, in payment of the interest and $10,000 on the principal. I trust that will not be too terribly disappointing to those who have made such an effort to exploit this transaction. I trust we will recover the remainder of that indebtedness, which is not denied, which is recognized and on which this payment has now been made, and this is the fact of the matter.

Zander was pleased, perhaps even exhilarated by his performance and what he considered a clear vindication of the entire housing program, but Zander had stirred up the rancor of the rank and file, and the methods he and his floor lieutenants used to maintain control exacerbated an already hostile reaction. The use of walkie-talkie radios by his aides stationed about the auditorium, for example, made a curious impression on the membership. Such a communication system, though not unusual in other unions—especially those run with an iron hand—was unusual for AFSCME, and the image created of what could be construed as simply a means to achieve increased efficiency caused bitter resentment.

On the afternoon of the third day Nicholas Zonarich, an organization director of the AFL-CIO's Industrial Union Department, spoke to the delegates. The IUD had supported AFSCME, both morally and financially, but it was well aware that the union's low per capita tax would continue to inhibit growth. Zonarich made this point, rather forcefully, and his comments were not universally appreciated.

> But Delegates, permit me to project to you a fair statement. I think that it is about time that you will be kind to yourselves and be kind to your union,

that you measure up to the responsibilities in this convention and recognize that you have an antiquated and an outmoded dues per capita structure.

Zonarich was greeted with a chorus of boos, which must have surprised him, since his comments about the dues per capita structure could hardly have sounded very controversial. The explanation is the members resented being lectured to by an outsider: it was bad manners, they thought, for an outsider, even an official of an AFL-CIO affiliate, to tell the union what to do.

Zonarich's position was made even less tenable by the fact that, as the Wurf forces made certain everyone realized, he was the father-in-law of Gayle Wineriter, Zander's director of organization.

ZONARICH (continuing): I accept those boos for the reason that the statement I am making is in your behalf and I am sure that if you are fair to yourselves and you make a proper evaluation to meet the needs of an expanding American Federation of State, County and Municipal Employee's Union, you are going to have to vote a dues increase in this convention.

Zonarich tried to continue in spite of more boos, and argued that AFSCME had one of the lowest per capita taxes in the entire AFL-CIO. Finally, exasperated with his reception, he retorted, "Now these are not just wild things I am making here to you. I have been around a little bit, too, and have been booed before." He said the things he suggested were based on experience with the trade union movement and that the delegates "might as well measure up to [their] responsibilities."

When Zonarich stepped down, Zander apologized for the reception his membership had accorded the IUD official, an act Wurf is convinced gave a hefty boost to his own eventually

97

successful campaign to overthrow Zander.

Wurf: *Zander never learned. He just didn't learn. It was ineptness more than anything else. When people boo, you apologize, but you don't, for crying out loud, become embarrassed with your own constituency. He seemed more concerned about his relationship with Zonarich than with his own people.*

Just as the membership seemed to want no part of an increase in the per capita tax, it also showed little enthusiasm for changing to a regional system of electing vice-presidents. In fact, the delegates had little interest in issues at all; they cared much more—surprisingly so, the Wurf forces felt—about the campaign for the presidency. Rather than a convention of issues debated on the floor, it became a convention of caucusing, as groups of Zander supporters met in various rooms and hallways, and backers of COUR did likewise.

By Thursday, the day of the voting, the mood of the convention was even more belligerent and seemed to be deteriorating. Lima, Zander's secretary-treasurer candidate, tried to hold a black caucus, but the blacks from New York would have no part of it, and one of their number, a woman, is said to have told Lima, "When I look at you, I don't see a black man, I don't see a white man, I just see Zander."

For his part Wurf was unhappy that the real issues—regionalism, the post of secretary-treasurer, the housing program—had been set aside in favor of what was becoming a battle of personalities. And he worried about his own candidacy, remembering that until a short time before he had been Zander's "big mouth," and that had no doubt irritated the membership.

Wurf: Not Even Free Beer

Some of our people thought we could win in Milwaukee, but those of us who knew better figured they had a fever. I didn't think we had a prayer of getting more than 10 to 20 percent of the vote.

Chapman, who wasn't in the running since he'd gone to work for the State Department, showed up in the balcony, nursing a broken foot. That was interesting, because a third camp developed. It was for Arnold but opposed to his secretary-treasurer candidate, Lima. Chapman, it was argued, could be a compromise.

It occurred to me the delegates might be leaping at straws, for the choice between Zander and Wurf was getting harder to make.

In any event, the election took place, and Zander was getting more heavyhanded all the time. His people were pushing delegates around, making threats, trying to buy votes. There was even a guy running around with a gun sticking out of his pocket. Maybe it was a water pistol, but it left a bad impression.

That night before the voting we put on a fish fry for the delegates, charging a buck apiece, and they even had to pay for their beer. We had a better turnout than Zander's people did, and at their party the booze was free.

On Friday, May 4, at shortly after ten o'clock the Election Committee reported to the convention: Zander had been reelected president of AFSCME, defeating Wurf by a vote of 1,490 to 1,085. A runoff was necessary for the post of secretary-treasurer because Chapman (who had left the State Department to return to the union), Lima and Morgan all finished without a majority of the votes cast. In the special runoff election Morgan withdrew in favor of Gordon Chapman, who then won easily.

Ames, who one day would become secretary-treasurer, offers this somewhat subjective account of Chapman's return to union politics:

In December 1961 Bilik, who was then president of the Cincinnati Central Labor Union and a delegate to the AFL-CIO convention in Miami, called Wurf in New York. He said Chapman was in

99

Miami and was making noises about running for office at our 1962 convention. We had, of course, had no contact with Gordon.

Jerry immediately called both Hastings and me and insisted that we meet him in Miami. Hastings couldn't get away, but both Jerry and I went to Miami. We spent two days meeting with Chapman. At the end of that time agreement had been reached that Chapman would immediately announce his candidacy for president and that Wurf would run for secretary-treasurer as Gordon's running mate.

Wurf then went back to New York, leaving me with Gordon to help prepare his press release. Within a few hours Gordon had changed his mind, deciding not to run—or at least to postpone any decision.

The second chapter came when shortly afterward Gordon again changed his mind and decided to be a candidate for secretary-treasurer. The arrangement was more elaborate this time; he was to resign from the State Department and go on the payroll of the State Employees Council 7 in Michigan, thus making sure that his membership was beyond challenge.

A caucus was scheduled in the midwest, attended by most of the COUR group plus Chapman and the top officers of Council 7, not previously considered a part of the COUR group. Once again plans were made for a public announcement—this time that Chapman intended to run for secretary-treasurer. On the final day of the meeting—after the meeting had, in fact, adjourned—Chapman again changed his mind. Meanwhile, in Lansing, the Council 7 newspaper was delivered to the post office. The page one headline indicated that Gordon had resigned from the State Department, had joined the Council 7 staff and was a candidate for secretary-treasurer.

Still later, as it became evident that a decision on a running mate for Wurf could not be postponed any longer, Wurf and Morgan, who was at the time working for the AFL-CIO's Committee on Political Education (COPE), met for a long evening with Chapman in Washington. At this meeting Chapman repeatedly assured them that he would not become a candidate for either office under any circumstances. Based on these assurances Morgan resigned from the COPE job, and his candidacy was announced.

Wurf won 43 percent of the vote, and the COUR group was stunned by its accomplishment. The dissidents' highest hopes had been for something close to 30 percent for their presidential candidate, to indicate the viability of their reform movement.

Later that day, still not quite comprehending the full meaning of its success, the COUR leadership participated as the convention defeated the regionalism motion by a vote of 477 to 401 (the motion would have allowed vice-presidents to be elected from and by regional districts), and then—in an obvious indication of dissatisfaction with international leadership—voted no, no and no again to any rise in per capita tax. The other issues—housing, the post of secretary-treasurer, administration proposals to grant all officers four year terms—were never brought to the floor.

The convention closed with an incredible and rather sad display. Once the rise to a dollar had been soundly defeated, Zander began to reduce the figure—first to 90 cents, then to 80, then by nickels, and each time the convention roared no to an increase.

101

Wurf: Milwaukee Post-morten

Once elected, Zander went for his per capita tax increase from 65 cents to a buck. It was the most critical event of the convention, an auction in reverse, as it was rejected nickel by nickel. Then Arnold made an incredibly stupid threat: "Put your money where your mouth is, Jerry Wurf," he said, making it clear he was bleeding over almost losing the election.

He even started comparing himself with Christ and claimed he was being crucified, prompting one joker to stand up and holler, "And who's the other thief, Arnold."

When you compare yourself to Christ right after having beaten a Jewish opponent—beaten him with less than all the moralities that attend a democratic election—you really turn off a lot of people. I don't believe he intended it to be anti-Semitic. He really thought of himself as a martyr, and the Christ comparison was a subliminal reaction.

I wanted to recess to meet with our leadership. I was convinced that in the hostile environment of the moment the per capita tax could not be raised. I was afraid it might even be reduced. The union desperately needed the money, and so I was hoping we could work something out. I requested a recess and Zander readily agreed. I turned to Father Blatz and said, "Let's get a few of our guys together for a quick meeting." But as we walked out into the lobby of the sports arena we were surrounded by dozens of other delegates shouting things like: "Don't sell us out, Jerry." Many of them had been Zander supporters, I'm sure, the day before. We came to realize right away that the only thing to do then was to adjourn the convention.

Roy Kubista came over and said that the Wisconsin delegates, all of whom had voted for Zander, were distressed and outraged. They said the best thing for the union would be to adjourn the damned convention. The motion was made and the vote was overwhelming, maybe unanimous, for adjournment.

Chapman double-crossed us, plain and simple. Up until the last minute he refused to run for office and said he would support Morgan and myself. Then without telling us anything he showed up in Milwaukee and started playing footsy with a few staff guys who were close to him.

One was this guy McCormack who hated Zander but was willing to be his phony secretary-treasurer and who nominated him for president. McCormack at the same time zealously backed Chapman, and suddenly we had three candidates for secretary-treasurer—Chapman, Lima and Morgan.

Zander would have taken anybody but Chapman, so we made a cold-blooded political decision: we withdrew Morgan, and Chapman got elected. What we did was hook up with Chapman—as we would do again later—not because we were admirers of his, but because he had some influence with some Midwestern conservative people who were not necessarily sympathetic to guys like Gotbaum, Bilik and Wurf, who all reeked of New York.

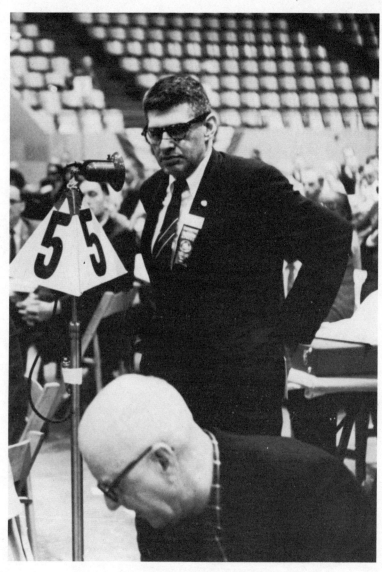

Contender Wurf at a floor mike at the 1962 convention

6.   Denver: A Difference of 21 Votes

Jim Newcomb of *The Milwaukee Sentinel* summarized the meaning of the 1962 convention, "Zander's triumph ended there." Newcomb's reasons:

- Zander's running mate, George Lima, was soundly beaten in the runoff by Gordon Chapman, former long-time secretary-treasurer who made a last minute bid for his old job while still an aide to Secretary of State Rusk. The vote was 1,583 for Chapman, 1,004 for Lima.
- Zander lost four of 11 vice president's posts to opponent Jerry Wurf's slate . . . .
- His plea for a 35-cent dues increase failed to win even a majority, and subsequent motions for 25, 15, and 5 cent raises also lost. A two-thirds vote was needed.

Zander's winning margin was more than 400 votes out of 2,575 cast, a three to two edge, but it was less than impressive to Wurf's supporters who realized that that was almost the exact number of votes controlled by international representatives. A pro-Wurf publication circulated by Council 8 in Columbus, Ohio ran an analysis of the vote under the headline: WURF POLLS 43% OF TOTAL VOTE IN BID FOR PRESIDENCY OF AFSCME. The story contained a report by the credentials committee that showed there were close to 100 international union staffers seated as delegates, representing nearly 300 local unions and councils and carrying more than 500 votes. "This was a substantial number of votes tied to the purse strings of the administration," the writer concluded.

As the COUR group began to study the votes, it was struck by how very close it had come to victory. The COURites decided that if they were to get their message to the membership, they would have to publish more and better newsletters and make all the personal appearances they could afford.

In the Zander camp a decidedly different strategy was adopted. Zander would remain above the fight and go back to union business, which included the housing program and international affairs, clearing the way for Kramer to direct union activities and internal politics. The next election was only two years ahead, and it soon became clear that Kramer's goal was to break the power of COUR.

Listed chronologically over the two year period, retaliatory actions included:

- May 1962—Illinois Local 1610 was put in trusteeship, and international representative Lillian Roberts was fired. (A trusteeship is a procedure by which the international president removes the officers of a local and takes control of the local's business affairs.) Both Roberts and Gotbaum, whose region included 1610, had opposed the administration in Milwaukee.
- September 1962—a new council (21) was chartered in Columbus, Ohio, and COUR charged it was in constitutional and jurisdictional conflict with Council 8 which had supported Wurf. An appeal to the executive board resulted in a favorable ruling for Council 8 against Zander's wishes.
- June 1963—the president of Council 55 in Lansing, Mich., protested to the executive board the shutdown of its newspaper and abolishment

106

of its legislative program.

- September 1963—Zander brought charges against Al Wurf, who was defecting to his brother's side. (The charges were general ones—mismanagement of fiscal matters and of the council and mishandling of the council's September convention.) In addition, Council 50 approved some proceedings of its Local 1516, proceedings which Zander labeled illegal and for which he placed 1516 under trusteeship. Wurf took the International to court over both the charges and the trusteeship and won both cases.

- October 1963—Council 55 was placed under trusteeship because COUR members supposedly had taken over the convention of the council.

- October 1963—The object of over 20 trivial charges leveled by an international union representative assigned to Illinois, Gotbaum was found guilty on only one of them and suspended from the union for 30 days, though he continued to direct the Chicago-Cook County Council throughout his suspension. Typical of the accusations was one that said Gotbaum had gone to a convention of Illinois Council 34 to try to persuade delegates to oppose Zander.

- January 1964—Council 55 agreed to hold a new convention (chaired by Leo Kramer) and was let out of trusteeship. Zander created Council 23 in the Detroit area to split off a substantial number of members he thought supported COUR.

- February 1964—Zander tried to take control of Council 50, Al Wurf's council, but met resistance and never carried it off.

The members of COUR charged repeatedly that the Zander administration was acting in bad faith in these disciplinary actions. Sometimes the membership could be con-

107

vinced, but more often COUR's complaints fell on deaf ears due to the respect the members still had for Zander and because of COUR's inability to prove just who was behind each action.

Meanwhile Leo Kramer was busy directing the internal politics of the union on Zander's behalf. Whether Kramer relished the job of political hatchet man, as some claim, or whether it simply fell to him as Zander's executive assistant and trusted ally, he worked at it zealously and tirelessly.

He began an informal mail poll of union leadership at the grass roots level, though he avoided calling on the leadership of COUR or its sympathizers. Each letter was a bit different, but the general theme was: what do you think of the opposition's chances, how effective is its approach and what can we do to counter the COUR program?

Although most responses were partisan and predictable, not all were welcome. Some were informative, reflecting the internal wrenchings of AFSCME in the year of the showdown.

An international staffer in the south responded by calling the COURites "false prophets and rumor mongers who spread trash (to) try to improve their position politically in our Union." He praised Zander as "our very fine Christian Gentleman and too-democratic President," and suggested the administration be more firm in laying down its policy for local union officers to follow. He closed by telling Kramer he hoped he had enjoyed his trip to Japan (where Zander had sent Kramer in the summer of 1963 as a representative to PSI).

Another international staff man reported from the field that he was worried about the effect the COUR campaign was having and was particularly concerned with charges of financial mismanagement being made against the administration by Secretary-Treasurer Chapman. "I was quite impressed with the sophistication of this last edition of COUR," he wrote. "Their approach and attack looks more reasonable to the uncommitted than they have in the past. And whether we like it or not, I do not believe Chapman's statements hurt them or him. If we allow it to go unchallenged, it may be to our disadvantage."

By September 1963 it was clear to at least one pro-Zander vice-president that COUR was making inroads:

> I am not convinced that we are fighting back as effectively as we might, but neither am I able to offer anything radically new that might serve us better. It would be helpful, I think, if the President could send out a periodic personal letter to the local union presidents addressing himself to these matters. Whatever personal contact he can make in the field is even better and he ought to devote what ever time he can in this effort.
>
> I have, however, in recent weeks become persuaded that we ought to get out of the housing business—at least until a little sanity returns to the internal relationships in our Union. I have not come to this conclusion easily, for, as you known, I have given the program whole-hearted support from its inception. Moreover, I feel terribly frustrated in having to give in on a fine program to such unreasoned opposition. The simple, brutal fact is, however, that we have been unable to excite the interest and support of our membership generally for housing. COUR had been concentrating its attack on this issue, I suspect because they find they are getting the most mileage out of it. I personally would like to continue our housing program—but I want more that Arnold Zander should continue as President of our Union. I do feel that we are being hurt politically on the issue. If Arnold still feels he wants to continue in housing, I'll no doubt stick by him on it. I do solicit his consideration of this view point, however.

The writer, Al Church, a Minnesota vice-president who

was to become a Wurf supporter after 1964, represented a growing attitude on the part of many officials: the housing program was more trouble than it was worth. One former headquarters staffer says today that the entire international staff, even Kramer, rejected the housing program.

Other responses to what COUR called "Leo's Letters" indicated heightening emotion, especially as convention time drew closer. One correspondent mentioned that he was getting comments from labor leaders in other unions as to the internal political problems of AFSCME, mentioned a rumor he'd heard that Chapman and Wurf might change places on the 1964 ticket and asked Kramer, "Any truth in you being a candidate for the Secretary-Treasurer's position? That might not be such a bad idea at that."

A field man in the South wrote:

> The membership who are not affected directly by this attack (COUR's newsletters) consider it a dirty business and will not get involved if they can help it. I know because I tried to get the Council to write COUR and ask them to take our people off the mailing list. Just that much caused some very bitter feelings. Some said that I was trying to get them into a fight that was not theirs. Others insisted that it was very much their fight and they belong in the fight. I could not get anything done.

He closed by suggesting "an avalanche of personal libel and slander suits against these individuals. If we start to cost them some of their own personal money it won't make any difference if we win or not they will slow down and others will be reluctant to take their place."

A vice-president of a local in the Midwest lectured Kramer:

> I think our International Executive Board and President Zanders (sic) are honest and sincere, but we all make mistakes. "He who makes no mistakes

110

does nothing, but he who makes too many loses his tail."

Leo, in closing let me say I can see both sides. I listen to the minority as well as the majority. Many a good point is lead by the minority. Always remember that the other man has a point also even if we don't agree with him. Also remember he may not agree with us, but we can accomplish something if we are serious and sincere.

Kramer's response, as contained in the historical files of AFSCME, was, in part, "It was very kind of you to write me that long, detailed and informative letter. Please keep in touch with me." The same man wrote to Kramer several months later in a more forceful tone:

I believe we need a more rigid program. You know several people have risen to fame, but few have stayed. John L. Lewis won by eliminating his opposition before election on some technicality, such as not paying back dues, or sending in per capita tax too late. He always comes up with an eliminating process. So does James Hoffa, and Walter Reuther. Zanders is going to have to find himself one in this game for there aren't any friends here. There is an old saying, "All is fair in love and war."

... Leo, I read both sides, COUR letters from opposition in Illinois. Any thing a bunch of Jews is for I am against, because if they cannot rule they will ruin and that almighty dollar if it isn't there they will take no part. We need some way to curb them, but no one will do it with our present Attorney General (Robert F. Kennedy).

According to the file, there was no response to this letter, perhaps because Kramer is Jewish.

111

One of Kramer's letters was received by a pro-COUR member of the executive board, John P. Caldwell of Missoula, Montana. His response, dated October 31, 1963, included a reference to an executive board action that was a setback for the housing program:

> It was difficult for me to divert my attention from collective bargaining to your report on what the Board did in October on housing, with the situation as tense as it was.
>
> I now see that your report omits the crucial decision of the Board to terminate housing until the Denver convention can settle the question of whether AFSCME ought to be in the housing business at all.
>
> You may remember that I mentioned the fact that housing diverts us from collective bargaining, and the experience Oct. 21, in Havre is an example, although trifling compared to the massive diversion at headquarters.

At its October meeting the board had made a decision to halt all housing projects until the question of the program's worth could be brought before delegates at the 1964 convention. The board's decision, opposed by Zander, was based on several events of the preceding summer.

In June 1963 a new project had been started in Madison, Wisconsin, just a few weeks before it was learned that the Puerto Rico project was in serious financial trouble. At the 1962 convention Zander had reaffirmed his faith in Fincke's ability to repay the balance of the $40,000 loan, but Fincke had not been able to make more payments. In the spring o 1963 Zander had filed suit against Transamerican Industries for the $30,000 still owed the union. Then on May 27 *The New York Times* carried a story announcing the bankruptcy of the development company, and on June 13 *The Milwaukee Journal* printed an account of the indictment of a Milwaukee

112

man who was the developer in the Puerto Rico project. Authorities in Massachusetts, where Transamerican Industries was located, were seeking the elusive Fincke on charges of fraud.

Neither the *Times* nor the *Sentinel* mentioned Zander or the union, but subsequent newspaper stories did, and COUR promptly reprinted them in its newsletter.

In August 1963 newspaper accounts of a new project in Malden, Massachusetts, began to appear when city officials learned of plans to hire a general contractor directly rather than advertise for bids. The city threatened to stop the project entirely. Favoritism is particularly objectionable to union members, and COUR made the most of it. The housing program had become the major issue of the campaign to the extent that whether Zander liked it or not, the executive board had no choice but to suspend it.

In late 1963 and early 1964 the COUR leadership intensified its campaign using the familiar issues: housing, international affairs and trips and the increasing number of international staff men being sent into the field, according to COUR to hold locals and councils in tow.

Wurf: Both the High Road and the Low

Kramer accused us of playing the high road and the low road at the same time, and in a way he was right, but what he called the "low road" was our effort to get our message across to the members at the local level.

On the one hand we stressed general issues intelligently and rationally, never impugning the Zander administration in any way. But at the local levels we would be handing out leaflets and holding meetings, dealing with specific indecencies that were being committed at headquarters: infringement of local autonomy, special arrangements and so forth.

We began mailing the Council 37 newspaper around the country. It told the story of a strong, capable, effective union, without getting into union politics, while the COUR newsletter

113

stuck with the broad, general issues of our international union political campaign: lack of organization, misuse of the union mechanism, the housing mess, international affairs, the heavyhandedness of national staff, the relinquishing by local unions of their right to self-determination and decision-making authority and so on.

In addition we made contact with people in the heartland, so-called Zander country, where we'd try to deal with local problems. Very often we found people who were new to our kind of thinking, who thought the anti-democratic practice was common, instead of understanding that under our constitution the authority to make decisions resided in local unions and councils, not in Washington.

In the course of the campaign one incident provided some comic relief, a dirty trick, so to speak, but small potatoes compared with campaign tactics of national political parties in the decade ahead. In January 1963 Kramer's book, *Labor's Paradox,* was published by John Wiley & Sons in New York. An employee of the publisher, in a hurry to obtain a photograph for the book cover and unaware of the internal fight of the union, called Council 37 instead of national headquarters.

Wurf's office happily cooperated, sending over a montage of public employees and union officials at work. The cover was prepared, and when the book was printed, an advance copy was sent to Zander in Washington. When he and Kramer examined the montage closely, they discovered in its center a picture, no larger than a dime, of Jerry Wurf.

They called Wiley and insisted the cover be changed. The publisher, who by then had bound 2,000 copies, at first refused but gave in when Zander offered to enlist the aid of the Fund For the Republic, which had commissioned Kramer's book as part of a series on internal trade union government. Wiley got another montage, replacing Wurf's photograph with that of a zookeeper washing down an

114

elephant. "I love to tell Wurf they replaced his face with an elephant's ass," Ames confides.

The story made *The New York Times,* and Kramer told his version of it in a general letter to the membership:

> Now I must also give credit to one story about the covers that is making the rounds. The tale goes something like this: the opportunity to get Wurf's picture on the cover was accidentally, of course, dumped into the laps of Jerry Wurf and his editor. Such opportunities don't walk into the front door every day and so, of course, they took it. The moral of the story is clear and so I need not spell it out.
>
> We have now come full cycle. Since the COURites and others could not get their pictures on the cover, they must now attack and smear the book.
>
> I am pleased that all the impartial observers and reviewers have said constructive things about the book. I have no illusions that I am a great writer, or even a good writer. The things that I had inside of me were what I had to say and I have said them. I have established a record for all to see. I am ready to let it stand up against those who sneak around the bars or use the telephone so the smut they spread cannot be proved against them. History will decide.

Kramer's letter was just one of many in a war of words that continued throughout the campaign. COUR used its news-letter more and more effectively to put issues before the rank and file; the administration countered with a series of "truth letters" by Ross Thomas, AFSCME public relations director.

Wurf: Opposition Game Plan

The Zander people had a two stage effort. First, they had the clout, they owned the machinery to influence delegates.

They were able, for example, to control the credentials committee. A letter from Sam Anonymous certifying that Bill Nobody was a delegate of Local X was accepted as a legitimate credential. They also spent very large sums of money, and I believe I can make a strong case that it came from the CIA and from housing developers.

Second, they tried to attack me in ways that were absolutely absurd. For one thing they claimed I wasted money, even to the extent of claiming I spent $800 for a chair in my office, one that cost $150 which I never did like. They even sent a photographer to get a picture of the chair, the only result being I then wasn't able to get rid of the damn thing.

They dug into my personal life pretty hard, and though they couldn't come up with much, there were all kinds of accusations. They told people that when I was single I dated lots of girls, and I pleaded guilty. At least I chased girls until I married Mildred in 1960. That marriage was the most important thing that ever happened to me, and Zander distressed Mildred and me very much by saying it was merely an attempt by me to achieve respectability.

They did other outrageous things. Some leaflets appeared, and though they could not be attributed to anyone, they had a professional touch. In one case the leafleteer, one of their staff guys in New England, emphasized my big nose in an amateurish appeal to anti-Semitism, and other leaflets depicted great ugliness in Joe Ames' face, which was badly chopped up in the war. That kind of thing doesn't go over in our union, and it was counter-productive to their effort.

Down south they circulated a picture of me handing a check to Roy Wilkins, head of the NAACP, and that was just stupid, because the one thing we were loud, clear and absolute on was how strongly we felt about the civil rights movement.

By the time of the 1964 convention the respective platforms of Zander and Wurf were generally well-known. The delegates, deluged with written material from both sides,

116

might not have had a clear idea of every nuance or fully appreciated every maneuver, but they knew Wurf was for regionalism and against the housing program and the amount of time and money spent on Public Services International (PSI) and international affairs, and that Zander was against regionalism and proud of the housing program and his involvement internationally. They knew Wurf was against any increase in presidential power and Zander wanted to achieve more centralized control at headquarters. The president still favored elimination of the elective office of secretary-treasurer, although he had picked the powerful and popular Bill McEntee of Philadelphia to run for the post on his ticket, and he would again seek an increase in the per capita tax.

The Denver Post described the situation on the eve of the convention:

> The vanguard of an estimated 1,200 delegates to the 14th biennial convention of the American Federation of State, County and Municipal Employees (AFSCME) began arriving in Denver Saturday.
>
> But unlike most convention-goers, the AFSCME delegates aren't meeting in traditional hale and hearty good fellowship.
>
> The organization is sharply divided into two camps, and voting delegates are eagerly recruited by followers of two leaders of the 250,000-member union, the 17th largest organization in the AFL-CIO.
>
> During the five-day convention, which opens Monday at the Denver Hilton Hotel, the meetings will, if recent history is a guide, resemble a partisan political convention.
>
> The two camps will monitor the meetings of all committees dealing with rules and procedures, credentials, resolutions and nominations of officers, for each accuses the other of improper and illegal procedure. Nominations are set for 10 a.m. Tuesday with elections about noon Wednesday.

The convention's opening session on Monday, April 27 lasted an hour and 45 minutes. It was devoted to Zander's opening address, a direct and aggressive speech. One by one he dealt with the opponent's main charges.

International affairs:

Our International work, carried on in the name of Public Services International, the PSI, has been expanded and strengthened without expense to the International Union either in money or employee time. There has been no diversion to it money-wise or staff-wise from the usual basic and historic program of the union. It has not caused any distraction from our ordinary work, while bringing to our union great credit for our part in the fight against Communism and backwardness. In this connection our success has been stellar . . .

Housing:

. . . The whole labor movement is now in that operation (housing). We are still out in front but no longer alone. The AFL-CIO asked that "the auxiliary housing corporation be widely publicized throughout the trade union movement." We already have our auxiliary housing in the form of our Development Fund with more than $120,000.00 in it. This $120,000.00 came from the sponsorship of these projects and not from any members' dues nor from any general funds of the union. In addition we own millions of dollars of property with appreciating values and without any investment in union funds or employees' time. There has been no distraction or diversion from normal union activities to the housing program, except by its critics.

Here is the outreach which results from a sense of belonging to the age-old providential trend toward equality. There is no pettiness in that

118

concept. It leads to broad, rather than limited objectives, to long-range, as well as immediate goals. One feels personal insignificance in contemplation of the long sweep of the trend, like a grain of sand on the ocean beach. At the same time, he gets from understanding it the courage to accept challenges and not to run for cover at the first sign of criticism.

We are not going to duck and dodge or whine, but go bravely on! We are going to stand up to the blasting attacks made on us and put them also in perspective. *You* must direct the Federation as to how it is to proceed during the next two years until we meet again, whether with courage and determinism or with fear and hesitation.

On COUR, with reference to Zander's allegation that another international union was threatening to raid AFSCME because of its internal difficulties:

One could easily think that the little group of ex-employees would be happy if this other union took us. Is this so inconceivable? Haven't they consistently aided and abetted every opposition to this union with lies, irresponsible propaganda, false charges and accusations published and distributed to the press, to Members of Congress and throughout the movement? By falsely charging that this administration used race hate and religious prejudice and that I am a Communist, are they not attacking the very life of this union and giving aid and comfort to the employers? Did not an employer say to one of our men, "Why should I deal with a bandit organization?" and produced the literature.

At a meeting in the mid-west, a spokesman of the little band of critics submitted a so-called "program." It consisted of a number of regional

119

directors, a smaller number of assistant regional directors, and that was all. Well, this convention must choose alternatives and I trust and am confident that it will not choose one like that . . .

President Woodrow Wilson said, "The President is at liberty, both in law and conscience, to be as big a man as he can be." Your President is at liberty, by both constitution and conscience, to think big thoughts, to love when others hate, and to plan beyond the means of the organization to perform . . .

We are for the age-old trend towards the development of equality. We are for a strong, national movement for peace and freedom. Now is the time for alignment with the providential fact of the development of equality which means our forward looking and responsible program.

I have been threatened with a bad convention, even worse than the last. But we don't have to put up with that. The delegates to this convention have it in their voices and in their votes to have a good convention. Last time many delegates went back home ashamed of the wasted opportunity. It must be different this time. Let us give serious consideration to important matters.

There is a time for righteous wrath. This may be that time. Let this convention be the one at which we do not tolerate the abuse of rights and privileges in order to delay and frustrate the will of the majority.

The election was virtually the only business of the 1964 convention. Since Walter Reuther was elected president of the United Auto Workers in 1946, no incumbent president of a major international union had been unseated by a protest or reform element in his union. Nor was there much feeling that it would happen in Denver. Although delegates and observers

Demonstration for candidate Wurf at the 1964 convention in Denver

alike expected the vote to be close, smart money was on Zander. Newspaper reporters, nearly unanimous that Zander would win, had a betting pool on his margin of victory.

Wurf: God Bless Mildred

Mildred got off the airplane in Denver, and I came down to meet her because I was bored with the meetings. Mildred is usually very diplomatic, but she comes from the West and there she was saying, "God, it's good to be in the West, it's just so much nicer than the East." I reminded her as politely as I could that my election depended on eastern votes.

At the convention Mildred was wandering around and some guy she didn't know started a conversation. "You know," he said, "I don't like this fellow Zander, but Wurf? I understand he has a reputation for being rough and loud, even profane. Do you know him? Is he a nice guy?"

Mildred says I've been misquoting her for years by claiming she said I wasn't a nice guy, but Zander wasn't a nice guy either. What she really said was, "Fortunately he isn't running for nicest guy. He's running to be president of the union, and for that job he is the best there is."

With the nominations set for Tuesday and the voting for Wednesday, the convention recessed early on the first day, and the electioneering began in earnest. While Zander was making his opening address, members of COUR had been furnishing the delegates with pamphlets charging the Zander administration with bringing 101 union representatives to the convention with all expenses paid by union dues, a cost estimated at $40,000. The pamphlets also accused the convention committees of not being "representative of the majority of the delegates at this convention."

Newspaper interest in the AFSCME contest was building. *The Rocky Mountain News* carried an account on Tuesday:

Wurf's "young turks," as they are described by

122

Zander, claim that the union has been weakened, not strengthened, by excessive centralization or international control.

Zander sees his theory of centralized strength as the salvation of the organization and the key to its continued and vigorous growth.

"Look," said a woman delegate from Detroit who was sporting a large pro-Wurf button, "it boils down to whether we're going to have one-man rule or democratic rule by the executive board."

She added, "He (Zander) goes along with the democratic idea when the board's in session, but when it's not, he thinks he alone is the union."

Zander himself hotly disputes this point. "Those people are interested only in taking over this union . . ."

Asked if he were certain of winning his 15th 2-year term, Zander replied "certainly." He smiled. "They haven't got a chance. It won't even be close."

"I'm still in good shape. They're going to find out there's some spunk left in the old man."

In the Wurf camp an aide declared flatly, "We're going to win."

Said another Wurf backer, "We're confident we can get 57 percent of the vote."

Sam Romer of *The Minneapolis Tribune*, a boyhood friend of Wurf's who had been following the AFSCME story for years, filed an exclusive story: "Zander has been criticized for retaining Martin K. Frank, a Washington, D.C. real estate broker and housing consultant, and giving Frank 25 percent of the 'organization fees.'

"Last year Frank received $71,000 as his share of the fees, in addition to a $15,000 retainer."

Wurf: *Romer is dead now, but he was one of the great labor reporters and a great guy. He did something during the*

123

convention I'll never forget. I was going crazy with the pressure of the convention, and he walked into the room one night and said, "Why don't I take you and Mildred out to dinner, get away from these sonsabitches." We went to Trader Vic's and talked about everything—our old socialist days, his experience in Spain during the civil war, and getting away from the goddamn convention was therapeutic for me. Sam was a hard nosed reporter who understood us better than anyone else.

From the time the delegates began arriving over the weekend, the two factions had been spending money for favors, errands, parties, meetings—whatever it took to get the message across. While Arnold Zander remained in his hotel room—he never approved of backslapping and buttonholing during elections—Kramer directed the administrative strategy.

COUR strategy was directed by Ames, although Wurf retained considerable authority. Other high level strategists included Bilik, Gotbaum, Hastings, Blatz, Chuck Svenson and Charlie Taibi of the District Council 37 staff, Schut and Mildred Wurf.

By the time the nominations were made on Tuesday the delegates were bleary-eyed from caucusing and cajoling and last minute attempts at persuasion.

The first nomination for the presidency was made by international Vice-President Steve Clark:

> . . . It is my privilege to place in nomination the name of the man who conceived and presided at the birth of this great international union. The man who has nurtured and guided it to a foremost position in the family of international unions.
>
> He is honest, sincere and dedicated to the economic and social welfare of public employees. He has demonstrated by deeds and actions that he is concerned for the welfare of our friends and neigh-

bors around the world. He believes that the international union is a mechanism that should be used to promote the welfare of our people above and beyond just the normal activities of the trade union . . .

It has been said that man is the master of his own destiny. I believe the destiny of this International Union and the welfare of its members can best be served under the leadership of our International President, Arnold S. Zander.

The next nominating speech was made by Delegate Albert Blatz, the Catholic priest who represented Local 614 of Minnesota:

Brothers and sisters, we are presently engaged in the serious task of selecting our leader for the next two years. This is our high privilege—our inalienable right—our solemn responsibility. We are completely free in our choice. Past service can and should be rewarded, not by perpetual re-election but by an adequate pension. No one has any claim on the presidency of this Union. This office is ours to bestow. We must not bestow it as a decoration to be worn on the lapel of the recipient, but as a burden to be borne in the best interest of our members. Dissatisfaction with the status quo does not brand one as a traitor or as evil. Rather, treason lies in being complacent in the face of mediocrity or worse.

With this preamble I offer for your consideration a man who will regard the presidency of this Union as a high privilege, a sacred trust, a golden opportunity to give of himself to further our common cause.

He will be our servant, not our master. He will return this Union to its members. On his desk will be a sign—the buck stops here.

He is a man pledged to throw open the windows to let in the fresh air of constitutional reform so necessary if we are to give anything but lip service to democracy. If our Union, or any union, is not democratic, it is an abomination . . .

Who is this man? And he is a man—not a god. He has his faults, but he has been much maligned. He has been accused of many things, but he has never been accused of complacency. He is a fighting man with the backbone and the guts this Union needs. I nominate the next president of this Union—the dynamic, young, fiery director of New York Council 37—Jerry Wurf.

On Tuesday afternoon while convention speeches were droning on, Ames was moving around the Denver Hilton doing some checking on his own, some potential vote counting. He was not pleased with what he learned. "On Tuesday there were literally dozens of caucuses," he later recounted. "A lot of them were 'little-man-with-the-power' caucuses where small councils would try to play the swing vote. And a lot of small councils were trying to cut it down the middle by endorsing Zander and Chapman, which would have been ridiculous. (Chapman, having split with Zander, was running for secretary-treasurer on the COUR slate, a liaison of convenience.)

Another thing that worried Ames was that he'd heard a rumor that Kramer had called a meeting, ". . . sometime in the afternoon or evening, supposedly, to see if they could get the election postponed for a day. I knew that our strength was ebbing, and if he could have pulled that off, they would have won it."

Ames was one of 11 candidates for vice-president on Wurf's slate, but he was concerned by the thought that Wurf's election might hinge on a small council from the west that was insisting that its candidate for vice-president be put on the slate.

126

He asked Tom Morgan, like Ames an expert at tallying prospective votes, to make an independent count. Morgan's count was almost identical to Ames'. "I knew what I had to do," he says. "I had to get off the ticket."

Ames withdrew, and he convinced John Zinos of Milwaukee that he too should pull out in favor of vice-presidential candidates who could deliver desperately needed votes to Wurf. Tuesday night the Wurf faction held a closed caucus from which even Wurf was excluded, and Ames and Zinos asked permission to withdraw. Their action was approved by the convention the next day.

The small council from the west (Oregon Council 75) that Ames figured could swing the election carried 34 votes (its own plus those of some allies), and its pro-Wurf vice-presidential candidate, Rena Ainsworth, was elected.

On Wednesday, April 29th the voting was held. As soon as the delegates had finished casting their secret ballots, the Elections Committee—under the supervision of the Honest Ballot Association—withdrew to count the votes.

That night Zander called Public Relations Director Ross Thomas to his hotel room and asked what he thought the outcome would be. Thomas, a veteran of several political battles during his career in the labor movement, said, "I don't think we're going to win." Zander then took a written message from his coat pocket, explained to Thomas that it was from his Christian Science reader and read, "The forces of good will triumph over the forces of evil."

In the Wurf suite the partisans were gathered to await the results. Fannie Fine, an officer of Council 37 in New York, was the contact within the Elections Committee. When the count was official, she would see that word got to the Wurf suite.

To assure security only Elections Committee members could enter the room where the votes were being counted. According to official procedure the results would not be known until they were presented on the floor the next morning, but according to tradition there would be a leak, and the result would be known around the hotel in minutes.

The convention banquet was scheduled for that night, and as the time for it grew near, the first leak, an inaccurate one as it turned out, occurred. Hastings, posted outside the counting room, was the first to pass the word—Zander had been reelected.

Bilik has a vivid recollection of what happened in the Wurf suite when Hastings' phone call came:

> I don't know who answered the phone, but whoever it was, he or she turned and said, "We lost by 40 votes." Now, everyone who had really worked was there—Ames, Gotbaum, and the Wurfs, a whole bunch of people. And total gloom settled over that room. I remember, it was very hot, and someone had lowered one of those large floor-to-ceiling windows down from the top. I looked over, and Vic Gotbaum was leaning on one, with his arms on the window. Gotbaum had really put it all on the line for Wurf. He couldn't go home again if Zander had won. And I got the most eerie feeling that he was going to jump.

The mood was simple despair. One man in the room shook his head and proclaimed, "Ah, the hell with this. I'm going to go out and join management and make some money." A group of big men, members of Laborers Local 924 (Wurf's home local), who had promised Wurf they would cause no trouble, saw the result as a grounds for nullifying that promise: "If they stole it, we're going out and find them." Jerry Wurf talked very fast, as his wife remembers it, and was able to calm the angry laborers. The Wurfs then left to go down to congratulate the Zanders.

Two minutes later, according to Bilik, the phone rang again. It was Tom Morgan who had just been given the correct count by Fannie Fine. Wurf had won by 21 votes.

128

"Get to Wurf," shouted Bilik. "Get him before he goes onto the floor."

Morgan, who then weighed nearly 250 pounds, grabbed Fannie Fine by the hand and started to run. "We caught Jerry," he recalls, "just as they were entering the room. I yelled, 'Jerry, you won. You won.' Wurf gave me the damnedest look and said, 'I can't take this. Please don't kid around. Where's Fannie?

Fannie Fine, a tiny woman, had been kept back by a number of bystanders who had formed a ring around the Wurfs. Finally she was able to tell Wurf the happy news.

The movement that had its genesis six years earlier in a heated series of exchanges had grown into a reform program, and a bitter factional battle seemed finally to be ending as members of COUR waited for the following day, when the victory that had seemed so difficult, so far away, would become official. But the factionalism and bitterness did not disappear in that single night of waiting, and the COURites had one more battle before their victory became reality.

On Thursday morning, a time of expected exhilaration for the newly elected officers and their supporters, Zander refused to call for the final report of the Elections Committee. Claiming it was not yet ready to report, he would not sanction the unofficial reports that were by then common knowledge.

The reason they were common knowledge was that reporters had observed the count with the permission of the Honest Ballot Association, Elections Committee and both sides. The morning paper carried a report of Wurf's victory and an accurate tally of the vote, so when Zander continued to delay the report of the Elections Committee, Wurf's supporters bought all the papers they could find and distributed them throughout the hall.

The scene threatened to turn into chaos. George Abrams, executive director of the Honest Ballot Association, appeared before the convention and said the election results were final and the committee should report. McEntee, Zander's running mate, agreed, so finally the Elections Committee chairman, John E. Murphy of Wisconsin, announced the results:

for president: Wurf, 1,450 votes; Zander, 1,429 votes;

for secretary-treasurer: Chapman, 1,566 votes; McEntee, 1,302 votes.

Murphy went on to give the results of the vote for the international executive board. Out of 11 vice-presidents, 10 were COUR supporters.

When the results were official and the demonstrations began, the man seated next to Mildred Wurf released her hand. He had been holding it for almost two hours in an effort to calm and reassure her. His name was Abe Zwerdling, a Wurf family friend and the former legal aide to a one-time president of the CIO. He looked at the wife of the new president of AFSCME and said, "You know, I did the same thing for another woman once. Her name was Mae Reuther."

Then Jerry Wurf addressed the convention:

PRESIDENT-ELECT WURF: . . . President Zander, Secretary-Treasurer Chapman, members of the International Executive Board, I am overwhelmed, pleased and breathless at the fact that you have chosen to give me this tremendous responsibility for this great organization. We have come through a long, arduous and sometimes unpleasant campaign as we sought—both sides sought—to make their feelings known on the issues, and I am afraid, on the personalities of the union.

I want to make the comment—and I want you to believe me, and more importantly I want you to see to it—that this Union, with Gordon Chapman and the incoming Executive Board, will be administered for all the members and all of the locals; I could not possibly care whom you voted for or whose button you wore or whom you campaigned for; we are all starting as of this moment. We are starting as responsible to one another, with the understanding

that our obligation and our solidarity with each
other is more important than the political
campaign that has just now come to an end.

After praising Arnold Zander and admitting his personal
and professional debt to him, Wurf continued.

We have a union with a multiplicity of problems,
and I wish that it were possible this afternoon to
pass enough amendments or enough resolutions to
solve these problems; we could not do that if we met
for two more weeks. The reason is because these
problems, in addition to being rooted in the
mechanics of our union, are rooted in many, many
frustrations, which spring from our relationships
with public employers, our relationships with the
labor movement and so on.

But I am ready to promise you that . . . we can
go forward in a united fashion, in a solid fashion, to
face the complex problems.

I want to assure everyone in this room—and I
know I speak for the incoming Executive
Board—that not only will the right to disagree and
the right to criticize be permitted, but as a matter of
cold, hard fact, it is only with this kind of disagreement, when it is responsible—this kind of criticism,
when it is responsible—that we can fulfill our obligations to each other and to the people who pay the
freight of the Union.

Basically, no set of elected officers can succeed in
performing their tasks unless they have the cooperation and assistance of the membership of this
union. And, with your help and God's help, I hope I
can face up to the task you have given me.

Thank you very much.

Mr. Chairman, I would like to move that this
Convention go on record that the President Emer-

131

itus of this International Union, Arnold S. Zander, shall receive his present salary, and emoluments of a car—I don't know them all; and perhaps some expenses—and a good parliamentarian will probably beat me to death with all of this, but generally speaking, that all of the economic perquisites attendant on the office of president be paid to President Emeritus Arnold Zander until such time as he shall reach the regular retirement age as fixed by the retirement system of our international union.

Shortly after Wurf began his term as president of AFSCME, Kramer and several others, on behalf of Zander, filed a suit with the Department of Labor to overturn the election. The suit was dismissed.

Various officers of the union, past and present, have offered explanations as to why Zander lost. One of the most cogent came from McEntee. "Arnold Zander had this wonderful thing, his own union. And it was like a great big apple just sitting there. But he turned away and didn't watch it, didn't take care of it. And things started to go wrong with it. And Jerry Wurf came along, and he had the ambition and the common sense to take advantage of it."

Wurf: Victory at Last

I have a quick temper which I sometimes refer to as my Donald Duck streak, and one thing that was understood at these conventions was that I had to keep quiet. For a guy like me that is painful as hell, but it was necessary. I remember not long before the Denver convention there was a meeting with Zander in Washington to decide our representation on the credentials committee, and before we went in Blatz gave me a long lecture about behaving myself and not losing my temper. Arnold chose that occasion to ramble on about his 28 glorious years in office and how moral and honest he was, exasperating Blatz to the point that he slammed his big fist down on the table and yelled, "Stop the pious bullshit, Arnold." Coming from a Catholic priest, that sort of startled Zander and broke up the meeting.

In any event, I was on my best behavior in Denver, which is just as well, for not only was it a very close election, it was a carnival of cockeyed events.

We were better prepared than the time before. We brought a mimeograph machine, and we got a room in the hotel for an office where we turned out our material, which I admit was pretty rough and amateurish. But that went over pretty well with the delegates who understood we didn't have fancy printing facilities.

There was a big Zander sign strung across the hotel lobby, and after a hassle we put one up too, only to have it cut down. But they left some string and tatters dangling, and we decided to leave them that way on the theory people would get the point.

They had packed the credentials committee again, seating every SOB in sight, and I was annoyed with Hastings who was a member of the committee. He'd done some nose counting and decided we were in such strong shape, it didn't matter. Nonetheless, there were "locals" seated by the committee that we never heard from or saw again.

Bilik was in charge of putting together our slate of candidates for the Executive Board. I didn't attend the meetings, but he used a democratic process in making choices that were the product of a consensus, determined by a series of meetings with delegates from each caucus.

The other side made its picks at a meeting of a few guys in Zander's room. That wasn't lost on the delegates either.

After the voting Mildred and I waited for the results in our room, along with a group of our supporters. Hastings was posted outside the door of the room where the Honest Ballot Association was in charge of the tabulation. A guy we called the one-armed bandit, a mean, unpleasant customer named John Zancanaro, walked out of the meeting and very cleverly

133

said to Hastings, "Well, you elected Chapman again, and you may win the board by a slight margin, but we croaked Wurf."

Maybe Bilik doesn't remember who answered the phone, but I do. It was I who took Hastings' call. He said simply, "Jerry, you got dumped."

I turned to the people in the room and told them what had happened. They were dejected, several of them cried. Gotbaum especially was terribly depressed. I told them it was tough luck, that I thought I'd done my bit and that I had finished fighting. It was time to go downstairs and congratulate Zander.

And then Mildred—good Christian, moral woman and all that—did a strange thing. With real dismay, in a way I'd never heard her speak, she turned to Father Blatz in the hallway and asked, "Do we really have to congratulate him?"

Frankie Carpenito, a member of my home local in New York, grabbed me in the hall. Frankie was famous for thinking that with a name like Blatz our good Roman Catholic priest could only be a Baptist. "Boss, you told us to be good and take all this crap but—excuse me, Father—goddamn it now we're going to do a little ball-busting around here."

We went down to the ballroom floor where a banquet was going on, and a group of our people were just outside the banquet hall screaming, "We won! We won!" And they tried to put me on their shoulders. I demanded, "What the hell are you doing? I know how to lose. I know how to win. But I can't stand this, so knock it off."

I was trying to control the profanity, because along with Mildred there were a lot of women there. Everyone was crowding around, while a couple of our New York guys were protecting Mildred who was having trouble with a disc in her back. In fact, Hastings got too close and was flattened against a wall like a cue ball.

Then Fannie Fine, a member of the election committee from New York, broke through the mass of confusion and yelled, "Jerry, don't you understand, we won. We won 100 percent down the line."

134

By then we were in the back of the room where the banquet was going on, and Blatz said, "We can't break up the banquet, so everybody get out of here."

The next morning Zander and a few of his hard-nosed followers tried to brazen it out. They knew I'd won, all the reporters knew I'd won, everybody knew I'd won. I had run into young Jerry McEntee, Bill's son, in the bar, and he was moaning, "Impossible, how did they do it?" As soon as his father saw me, however, he congratulated me and assured me of his support.

But Zander wouldn't let the committee report, and by then even his own supporters were kicking up a fuss. Finally the guy from the Honest Ballot Association got up and established the fact I had won.

Then Bill McEntee came up to me and said, "You know, Jerry, Zander's got to stop this nonsense or it is going to tear up the Union." It was McEntee, Zander's running mate, who later asked me to keep Zander on at full salary until retirement. I did the best I could for Arnold, for I am a confirmed believer in human dignity, and the healing process for the union had to begin with a measure of dignity for Arnold Zander.

Unable to conceal his disappointment, Zander acknowledges Wurf's victory at the 1964 convention in Denver

7.   Making Good on Campaign Vows

We regret to find wholesale disregard of legal re-
quirements both in the inception and subsequent
management of these projects, ranging from failure
to file financial reports to filing false ones, from im-
proper commingling to possibly criminal siphoning
of corporation funds . . . We see no alternative to
pursuing these matters to solution.

Joseph A. Klausner and Raymond Buchbinder
(Buchbinder, Stein & Co., Auditors)
The Second Interim Report on Housing to
AFSCME's Executive Board, Oct. 24, 1964

While the delegates to AFSCME's 1964 international convention assembled in the hall on Thursday, April 31 to hear
the Elections Committee's final report on the presidential
race, a COUR delegation arrived in Washington, D.C. after a
midnight flight from Denver. Bob Hastings, who was to be
President Wurf's executive assistant, led the advance party to
AFSCME headquarters where, as soon as Wurf's election was
confirmed, it took control of the books and began to set the
union's house in order.

What Hastings found was shocking. Books and files were
in general disarray, poorly kept and incomplete. All the
union's files on special arrangements were gone. Similarly,
the books for the dozen-odd housing corporations set up by

137

Zander and Frank were in disorderly condition. The team had come to Washington mainly to keep anyone from tampering with certain important files, but there were very few files, and in the case of some housing corporations no books had been kept at all.

The new president and his wife Mildred arrived in Washington on May 2, the day following the convention, and took a room in a hotel close to the international offices. When Wurf arrived at headquarters, he found a situation which he described as "dreadful . . . administratively and organizationally." The physical condition of the building itself was poor—there was debris and broken glass on the lawn, and several large lights outside the building needed to be replaced. Members of the old staff were in the offices, not knowing what their role in the new administration would be or what to do until they knew.

Hastings was put in charge of restructuring and repairing the international staff, and Morgan was made director of organization. *Life* magazine said in 1966 that it was Wurf's immediate handling of the staffing problem, his "willingness to clean out dead wood," that "soon earned him a reputation for toughness."

There were some big trees in the dead wood forest, for the only major Zander staff member who offered his resignation immediately after the election was Ross Thomas. Leo Kramer and Gayle Wineriter did not. They were at headquarters when Wurf arrived.

There had been an attempt on the floor of the convention to get an amendment passed to protect the jobs of international staffers, but it failed. It was well known that Wurf considered the large international staff a heavy financial burden on the union and that cutbacks were essential.

Kramer asked to be kept on in some capacity, however, and for a while he was. But he, Wineriter and others resigned within a few weeks. In August Kramer and Henry Wilson, AFSCME's former general counsel, accepted positions with the

Laborers International Union—Kramer as a director of organizing activities in the public employee field and Wilson as assistant to the general counsel.

Wurf: Picking Up the Pieces

One of the first things I did when I got to Washington was to ask George Meany for a meeting. Someone told me later I didn't make much of an impression when I came in with Chapman, whom Meany regarded with a jaundiced eye. Meany said to me, "I've known Arnold Zander for 20 years, and he never was a trade unionist."

Earlier, while I was sitting in the anteroom waiting to see Meany, a guy who was on the staff at the AFL-CIO came up, kind of snickered, and asked, "Here with your tin cup, Jerry?" I didn't know what he meant then, but I soon discovered that our union had a reputation in town for not paying its way, for can-shaking. I made a quick decision to change all that. We sold the union headquarters, we took out some loans and we tried to make it clear that we would take care of our own financial affairs.

Kramer and other key people were still working at headquarters; only Ross Thomas had resigned. They wouldn't go, though it was clear they couldn't stay, and finally I figured Kramer and Wineriter and a few others were in this conspiracy with the union lawyer, Wilson, to deliver all or part of the union to the Laborers. That was where we parted ways.

I also discovered that the financial report they distributed at the convention was phony. It didn't show about a quarter of a million dollars of our liabilities. It was clear we were in terrible trouble, in fact we were broke, and the building showed it—broken glass, garbage and debris all over the place.

We never could reconstruct the books on the housing program because they were in such a mess. Here we had millions of dollars invested in housing, and nobody knew anything about it.

139

The staffing problem, though immediate and preliminary to a thorough housecleaning, was relatively minor in regard to the overall task that faced the new administration. COUR's reform program had now become the union's mandate, and the new administration was charged with eliminating special arrangements, dealing with the housing program and developing a more democratic, regional voting system. In a report on the state of the union to the first executive board meeting in June 1964 Wurf put first priority on special arrangements:

> A most serious problem faces us in the field. It concerns local union autonomy and the conduct of some former international staff representatives who have attempted to take over councils that had been administered by them under special arrangement. We are taking steps to return these councils to the members.

The attempt of ex-Zander-controlled international staffers to solidify their power within those councils where they had formerly retained control due to special arrangements or trusteeships forced Wurf and the executive board into deliberate action. While they were moving to reduce the number of special arrangements, they had to place several locals and councils under trusteeship. Still, by the time of the next regular convention in 1966 the new administration had ended over 40 special arrangements, leaving only two—in Utah and Puerto Rico—in effect.

In his first address to the executive board Wurf also noted the need for constitutional reform, and the board appointed a Constitutional Revision Commission to study the constitution and recommend changes. Ames was named chairman of the commission, which reported to a special constitutional convention in 1965.

Wurf did not take up the housing program at the June 15 meeting because the investigation by Joseph Klausner, a lawyer, and Raymond Buchbinder of the auditing firm of Buchbinder, Stein, & Co., was incomplete. The board did, however, authorize further investigation and directed Wurf to develop a plan to discharge the housing program in a manner least harmful to the union.

The auditors may not have had enough time to complete their investigation, given the condition of the books and the absence of the people who kept them, but they found out enough to raise serious financial and legal questions and to rate the situation as "grave." They called the books kept for the AFSCME housing corporations (three in California, four in Wisconsin, two in Puerto Rico, one each in New York and Massachusetts and two more pending approval in Puerto Rico and Nebraska) "at the very least unprofessional." They found the project costs had been deliberately inflated for presentation to the Federal Housing Authority to secure loans, and in some cases falsification seemed to be aimed at appearing to conform to FHA guidelines while not actually doing so. They found possible kickbacks from builders, suspicious loan procedures and spurious land deals in which the corporations would pay inflated prices to developers.

Though Zander, Kramer and Frank had served as officers of the corporation, the report concentrated on Frank, who as housing consultant for the union as well as treasurer-attorney for the various corporations had received payment for his work beyond federal guidelines and executive board approval. The auditors were careful in their imputations, however, for several reasons. They felt the loose bookkeeping of the corporations (which was not centralized and allowed everyone down to the secretarial level to draw checks on AFSCME's development fund as well as on corporation funds) might simply be the result of carelessness rather than malfeasance. And both Zander and Frank insisted that they had acted with FHA knowledge, tacit approval and at times even implied encouragement. Though the auditors felt the defense was shaky, they advised the executive board: "To us it seems

141

that the surest protection is to ascertain the views of the competent public authority," meaning the FHA and other federal agencies involved.

By the time Buchbinder, Stein & Co. made its second report to the executive board in October 1964, its investigation had been sufficiently thorough for it to change its description of what had been a "grave" situation to one of "emergency proportions." The "highest government authorities" had denied they had either known of or condoned the practices the auditors described in their first report. The federal housing commissioner had instructed AFSCME's auditors to assume administrative responsibilities to rectify conditions inconsistent with union policy and good business practice and had ordered his own independent investigation into possible criminal acts. The federal agencies expressly disapproved of the following disclosed acts of the former union administration and its housing program:

- inflated claims of organization expenses
- kickback donations from builders
- inflation of land prices to reimburse builders for their kickbacks (in one instance—in Madison, Wisconsin—the builder bought the land for $108,920 and resold it to AFSCME within two weeks for $185,000)
- misstatements of financial conditions to conceal outstanding obligations to builders
- overstatements of construction costs to induce larger government loans or insurance than would otherwise have been allowed.

Among the most disturbing of the auditors' findings was that Zander and Frank had done business in the name of the union days after Zander had lost the election and Frank had been fired, and when they did finally leave, the union was liable for large sums of money it might not be able to pay. According to the report Zander was apparently trying to get

142

the housing program transferred to his private control and to cover up his involvement, while Frank withdrew funds from the union's holdings without approval or legal right and refused to return the money, insisting it was owed him.

After the executive board had reviewed the second interim report at its October 1964 meeting, it passed a resolution that read in part:

> ... and Whereas, the (board) is concerned lest certain matters contained in (the two interim reports) seriously affect the welfare of the union, but feels that fairness demands that the (board) give president Zander the opportunity to present his views on these matters ...
>
> It is hereby resolved: that the (board) appoint a subcommittee of three members to meet with the President Emeritus to inquire concerning the housing projects of the Federation and other matters ...

The resolution further stated that the subcommittee would specifically inquire about the formation and administration of the housing program and Zander's actions that bore upon his relations with the international union between April 30, 1964 and the time of the resolution. If offered Zander information about the nature of the reports, time to prepare adequately for the inquiry and right to counsel at his own expense.

The meeting was held in December. Zander appeared with his attorney and was generally unresponsive to questioning. Though the resolution had been printed in full as part of the story on the executive board meeting in October, there was no mention of the meeting in *The Public Employee,* and no charges were brought against Zander by either the union or the federal agencies. Neither the union nor the government was interested in airing its dirty laundry in public.

143

While the two reports were being compiled and the investigations undertaken, the Wurf administration began moving to disengage AFSCME completely from all housing projects. Both Wurf and Hastings have since mentioned the federal housing agency's reluctance to cooperate with their attempts at first (because of the great difficulty of finding nonprofit sponsors) until threatened with a public scandal by the new union administration, although a scandal was the very thing the union wanted to avoid. The only recourse was to find another sponsor to take over the projects.

In Puerto Rico that sponsor was the Puerto Rico Housing Authority. In July 1966 Hastings led an AFSCME delegation to the commonwealth to make the transfer. He called it the "funniest goddamn experience of my life."

AFSCME was willing to hand over to the Housing Authority for nothing two completed projects and a third awaiting approval, though they would be worth millions of dollars to the government and builders alike. But the builder, involved in a complicated kickback arrangement that baffled even the auditors, Buchbinder & Stein, refused to approve the offer. Perhaps partly because of a contract with the builder, but apparently for other reasons as well, the Housing Authority's lawyer also refused the offer and insisted that AFSCME officials negotiate with him. Without knowing they were involved in an elaborate face-saving process but beginning to understand the rules of the game, Hastings and the others sat down for a day and a half bargaining session with the lawyer. "We made absurd, ridiculous demands of the Authority, and the lawyer fought us every inch of the way," Hastings recounted. When the lawyer had saved enough face and proved himself worthy of his position with the Housing Authority, he settled with AFSCME in "an absolutely splendid agreement" in favor of the authority.

Unloading the projects within the continental United States proved more difficult. The projects themselves could not be considered highly valuable. Those in Milwaukee,

144

Madison, Watts, Malden and New York had been poorly maintained, and though some were not yet two years old, they were all badly in need of repair. All but one of the projects were segregated, and rent collection and management in general had been irregular and suspect.

AFSCME looked for a sponsor throughout 1964 and 1965 without luck. Then toward the end of 1966 it began to negotiate with the American Baptist Home Mission Society. The transfer of all nine remaining projects was agreed upon, effective November 29, 1966, and made official by the approval of the executive board at its January 1967 meeting. Such was the feeling of relief over unloading the projects that when Wurf proposed selling out to the Baptists for one dollar, the good Catholic Father Blatz proclaimed emphatically, "Mr. Chairman, they deserve it. I so move."

AFSCME had succeeded in shedding something that was at best a white elephant in a way that kept the union free from scandal, but the whole problem did not end there. The FHA, as a result of its independent investigation, barred Frank from the construction business. He appealed, was reinstated for a while and then barred again. He and W. Clay Jackson (a contractor for the Puerto Rican projects) brought suit against AFSCME for slander and defamation of character, involving the union in a court battle that continued for years. The last suit was dismissed in 1973. Wurf maintains these suits were brought by Frank and Jackson because they had been blacklisted by the housing agency. The lawsuits, Wurf claims, gave the FHA an excuse for continuing to deal with them.

Wurf: Getting Out of Housing

We hired Klausner to look into the housing program, and he wrote a devastating report. The whole thing was fraught with corruption. It did nothing for the union, and all sorts of people were making money out of it except our members.

Arnold Zander came to me and proposed that the union put its imprimatur on a nonprofit corporation that he and his wife, Lola, would run. This corporation, they proposed, would continue to back the housing program. I rejected the idea out of hand and vowed, if necessary, to fight it in court.

When the report on the investigation was put before the executive board, Father Blatz suggested Zander be offered an opportunity to appear before a special committee of the board to face the serious charges against him. Zander came before the committee, but he refused to answer questions, explaining he feared criminal charges. The last thing we wanted was to see Arnold indicted because the union didn't need that kind of notoriety. We didn't press Zander further.

At Klausner's suggestion we went to HUD where we met with a couple of top officials who had been deeply involved with Zander and Frank. They made the most absurd kind of defenses for the sort of practices the report revealed. Secretary Robert H. Weaver himself told me he really didn't give a damn if there were decencies or indecencies, proprieties or improprieties, honesty or dishonesty. He made it clear that the one thing he learned in all his years in public life was how to protect his ass.

Following Wurf's election, AFSCME began to deemphasize its role in international affairs. The union continued its affiliation with Public Services International, but relations were not what they had been under Zander. As one of Zander's last official duties and at his own request, the president emeritus was sent to a PSI international conference shortly after the Denver convention. Word got back to AFSCME headquarters that Zander had attacked Wurf while at the conference, promising European trade union leaders he would be back in power soon.

There were other implications of the international involvement that were mysterious and potentially dangerous. When Wurf first arrived at AFSCME headquarters following the '64 convention, he noticed the presence of what he describes as "trench-coat types." One of these men was

146

AFSCME's alternate representative to PSI, Howard McCabe. When the new president tried to find out from McCabe and his associates exactly what they were doing in the building, he received vague explanations, and he was advised to be patient and wait for the proper time to ask questions. Wurf and others in the COUR group had heard rumors of an AFSCME relationship with the Central Intelligence Agency, even of the possibility that CIA funds had found their way into the effort to reelect Zander. Late in the summer of 1964 the truth of some of these rumors came out.

Between the years 1958 and 1964 AFSCME had used CIA money for international operations. McCabe reportedly was a CIA agent who used his position as international representative to PSI to funnel money into anticommunist movements within the European trade union movement, to run guns to certain Latin American countries and to back favored political regimes and parties.

Just when, where, how and from whom Wurf found out about CIA activity in the union is a subject about which Wurf in intentionally vague. Apparently there was a clandestine meeting of some kind in the Washington area, and a request was made of Wurf that he allow the CIA to continue acting through AFSCME.

Wurf was caught in a dilemma. On the one hand he was genuinely concerned for the security of the United States, for he was a staunch though not fanatical anti-Communist. On the other hand he did not particularly support CIA activities and had rejected the idea of government involvement in the union movement—particularly a public workers union where government is "boss." Based on the need to keep government and union separate, he made his decision: he would not disclose the CIA's minglings in the affairs of AFSCME, but he would not allow the arrangement to continue.

It proved to be an auspicious decision because in early 1966 *The New York Times* revealed that the CIA was involved with two major unions in addition to AFSCME, the American

147

Constitution Revision Commission at a hearing, from left, Vivian Moore, commission secretary, Eric Polisar, special consultant, Joseph Ames, chairman

148

Newspaper Guild and the International Oil, Chemical, and Atomic Workers. The Newspaper Guild had used CIA money to run seminars and training programs. The Chemical Workers had used it to provide logistical support to unions of Latin American oil refinery workers. The money had come to them through so-called philanthropic foundations.

While the internal house cleaning was progressing at AFSCME headquarters in Washington, Ames was talking to officials and rank and file members around the country gathering information he needed to prepare a revision of the union's constitution. The Constitutional Revision Commission of which Ames was chairman had eight other members, John Boer, William McEntee, Lyman Penning, George Hammond, Norm Schut, Olive Beasley, Jack Brickner and Robert Oberbeck—a cross section of original COUR members, Zander loyalists and middle of the roaders. The late Eric Polisar, a professor at Cornell University and close friend of Jerry Wurf, played a major role as an advisor to the Commission. He attended all the hearings with Ames and was instrumental in the wording of the preamble.

In an effort to provide local union members with a chance to discuss their views on both the constitution and the structure of the union, the commission held hearings across the country in September and October 1964. In *The Public Employee* it urged members to attend, and announcements were placed in local newspapers. Commission members took turns chairing the meetings, but Ames was the driving force behind the commission's ultimate success.

Originally the commission intended to put together a draft revision of the constitution by early 1965 and circulate it to the executive board and local unions for study, the approval to come at the 1966 convention. But as the hearings got underway and the commission began to assess its efforts, a special constitutional convention, to be held in 1965, appeared to be in order despite the costs. The executive board acted at its January 1965 meeting on the commission's recommendation that a convention be held, and it was set for late May in Minneapolis.

Wurf: *I happen to think the convention was one of the most significant things that happened. Just one year after the fight ended the same people who had been tearing each other to pieces were working together in a spirit of unity and warmth, a spirit that was so necessary at a difficult moment in the history of the union.*

The board agreed to limit the convention to consideration of proposed amendments to the international constitution, which in effect meant the replacement of that constitution with a new one.

The new constitution that Ames—through what Wurf later called "a diligent, almost heroic effort"—managed to engineer and bring before the special convention dealt with the voting system and regionalism, the two positive mainstays of COUR's reform program, but it contained other changes that were acceptable surprises to the delegates.

One of the most significant innovations was the establishment of a seven member judicial panel to act as the union's "supreme court." The panel was to be elected by the executive board, so members of the board were prohibited from serving on it. Depending on the nature of a case, one or more panel members would conduct hearings and hear appeals. In the hearings the accused would be granted the same rights he would have in a court of law: to retain counsel, hear charges beforehand, submit a brief in his defense, question an accuser, present witnesses and refuse to testify against himself. Innocence would be presumed and safeguards provided that no member would be tried by someone biased against him.

The new constitution also enlarged the international executive board from 13 to 18 members. Added representation was necessary because of the new regional system of election and new voting structure based on size. Sixteen legislative districts were established, each to elect a vice-president. They

150

consisted of Northern New England, Southern New England, New York, Eastern, Mid-Eastern, Southeastern, Central, Michigan, Wisconsin, North Central, Mid-Western, South-western, Rocky Mountain, Northwestern, Western and Caribbean. The president and secretary-treasurer still were to be elected at large.

The most controversial item of the new constitution was revision of the voting system to the one proposed by COUR at the '62 convention. It stated that locals were entitled to votes on the basis of one per each 100 members (or fraction of a hundred) up to 400, and an additional vote for each thousand or fraction of a thousand members over 400. What made it controversial was that some delegates felt the system now favored large urban councils over small rural locals, a reverse of the situation under Zander.

Other points included in the new constitution were:
- a bill of rights which prefaced the constitution and provided for freedom of speech;
- unrestricted access to financial and other information concerning the operation of the union;
- the right to vote, run for and hold office;
- an election code providing strict impartiality in its application to all candidates, refusing candidates the use of union funds and disallowing endorsement of any candidates by official union publications;
- a limited ability to impose trusteeships under certain conditions, to be reviewed by the judicial panel within 30 days.

Although the points seem basic, they represent one of the most progressive union constitutions in the American labor movement.

In sharp contrast to the acrimonious conventions of '62 and '64, the special convention of '65 was orderly and productive, though the delegates were hardly in unanimous agreement on the provisions of the new constitution. The convention, attended by 600 delegates, was smaller than regular conventions, though they represented larger areas of power within the union. Several ex-Zander loyalists were there, and they and other rank and file delegates vocally objected to some parts of the new constitution. The major objection came over the reformed voting system. Sam Kinville of the Washington State Council of County and City Employees, Council 2, objected:

> Again, Mr. Chairman, and fellow delegates, section 7 is a drastic change . . . you will notice a proportionate basis . . .
>
> My point is—incidentally, I represent a small local union—the locals affiliated with our council are relatively small local unions. The largest local would be in the neighborhood of 400.
>
> It is true that you are not taking anything away from the small, local unions; they still have the one vote. But, in effect, you are giving more votes to the larger local union . . .
>
> We would argue this. We would say to you that the large local unions are more adequately represented in the Convention. You think with me, if you will, a large local union, the delegate from a large local union or the officer, is probably a little more capable than the guy who is officer or delegate from the small local union.
>
> First of all, he has had a little more competition to get up there. Certainly, I think most of you who have been in these conventions before realize that the articulate, the leadership of these conventions, by and large come from the large local unions.
>
> We would certainly have some objection to the proposition that the large local unions are not adequately represented. They are adequately represented. We would say to you that this International Union, after all, was built on small local unions.

Wurf: *Bill McEntee had come over to our side, and he was sitting next to me on the platform. Every time anything controversial came up, he'd say to me, "Recognize Kinville." Kinville was the spokesman for a small council, one with about 2,000 members, and he was on his feet about every five minutes. He was a diehard whose efforts were counterproductive; in fact he was an asset to the new union administration.*

There were other points of disagreement over words and phrases, and some minor changes were made, but for the most part the constitution was approved as it was presented, the reform voting system intact. Only on a rare occasion did a note of the old bitter factionalism creep in, as when a delegate, toward the end of the convention, accused Ames of twisting his statements: "Part of our problem is we make a statement, and by the time I get back to my chair it is twisted around a little bit by the chairman of the commission."

The constitution was approved by a clear two-thirds majority.

By the time of the new administration's first regular convention in April 1966, the COUR program of reform was complete. Due to cuts in international staff and dropping of the housing program, the public scandals which threatened had been avoided, and the union had moved from near bankruptcy to operating in the black. Most of the special arrangements had been stopped, and the constitution had been rewritten.

By and large the reforms rectified complaints and carried out promises of COUR during its campaign. Other reforms, more positive ones, were longer-lasting, though less tangible. There was, most importantly, the promise of a new kind of leadership, more aggressive and militant, dedicated to trade union principles and practices.

With an emphasis on harmony the election at the 1966 convention returned Wurf and his COUR associates to office for another two years. And in the spirit of that harmony the new leadership of 1966 included some old Zander lieutenants.

153

McEntee was elected vice-president from the Eastern District, and Steve Clark, the man who had nominated Zander in 1964 but who had since become a strong supporter of the new administration, was picked to represent the Wisconsin District.

Victor Gotbaum, executive director of District Council 37, on the picket line during New York City welfare employees strike in 1965

8.   The New Militancy: A National Issue

*The sound doctrine of public employment rela-
tions is one that assures and guarantees a reasonable and fair procedure—with independent third
party determination if necessary—for settling new
contract disputes and which, therefore, does not include the right to strike.*

Secretary of Labor W. Willard Wirtz
April 25, 1966

*We have said that we don't want the right to
strike just for the privilege of walking around the
building. But we don't think that the government
can give or take away the right to strike . . . So long
as workers sit at a bargaining table, they must have
something to deal with, something that will impress
the boss.*

Jerry Wurf
April 25, 1966

Wurf: *I had invited Secretary Wirtz to address our convention. He agreed but said he would just make some informal remarks. Instead he proceeded with a carefully worded
diatribe, a prepared statement, about public workers not having the right to strike. I was sort of annoyed, even though I
had then and still have very warm admiration for Bill Wirtz.*

155

It looked as though Wirtz was leaving, so I said, "Wait a minute, Bill. I'm about to say some things I want you to hear." The delegates loved it.

The Wurf-Wirtz encounter at the 1966 convention in Washington, D.C. was interpreted by the labor press and general media as a sign of growing militancy among public workers. "The Public Employees Ask for a Better Shake," headlined *Business Week,* and *Life* discovered Wurf to be a dynamic exception of youthful restiveness among a labor leadership grown old, reactionary and self-satisfied.

Once again, as in the early days of public employee unionism, the sides were lining up. Government employers could no longer rely on traditional attitudes toward public employment to deter a union's effort to achieve better wages, hours and working conditions. Nor, in fairness, did they wish to. Public employers were beginning to accept the notion that public and private workers should be treated equally. But it was a question of how equally. And the line was being drawn in almost all states and cities over the right to strike.

Not only were employers hardened by their philosophical bias against public employees' right to strike, but they also worried about the rise to power of leaders like Wurf who had reputations for being trade unionism militants. In the two years since Wurf's election AFSCME had been touted as representing a "new breed" determined to revolutionize public employee unionism. Wurf's personal reputation for aggressive militancy was now being reflected in the new mood of the American Federation of State, County and Municipal Employees. The union was changing, and employers in city halls, county offices and state houses across the country were not necessarily pleased. Conflict was inevitable.

By the time of the 1966 convention AFSCME had done much more than rewrite its constitution, instigate reforms and set its house in order. It had begun to practice the trade union principles that the delegates had approved as a better course for the '60s and '70s. AFSCME was getting results and a good deal of attention.

156

In 1962 President Kennedy had issued Executive Order 10988, establishing the machinery for union recognition and limited collective bargaining for civilian employees of the United States government. The order was a welcome boost for a public employee labor movement that had suffered the postwar reaction of such legislation as an anti-public unionism law in Virginia, Michigan's Hutcheson Act, New York's Condon-Wadlin and the nation's Taft-Hartley. A broad interpretation of the Kennedy order could have created an immediate demand by state and local public employees for the same rights as federal employees. But the old leadership of AFSCME had not taken advantage of the Kennedy order nor realized the great potential for organization provided by the large growth of state and local government jobs.

The new leadership exploited both. At almost the moment Wurf became president the union had begun pushing hard for collective bargaining laws or some form of favorable state legislation, and by the end of 1965 there were several such new laws. And within two years of Wurf's election the membership had been increased by 50,000.

Three new public employee bargaining laws were signed by state governors within a single month during the summer of 1965. Connecticut agreed to bargain collectively with municipal employees, Delaware with state and municipal employees and Michigan with local government and state employees not under civil service. That same year Massachusetts passed a collective bargaining law for its government employees, and Minnesota agreed on a legal requirement to "meet and confer" with state and local government employees.

Early in Wurf's first term, while the internal reforms were still being implemented, AFSCME became involved in a major strike. On January 4, 1965 more than 7,000 New York City welfare workers, members of AFSCME Local 371 and the independent Social Service Employees Union, walked off their jobs when the city refused to negotiate a new agreement. Wurf went to New York at the beginning of the strike to bring the

157

full weight of the union behind the workers' demands.

The city invoked the Condon-Wadlin Act, and Wurf announced that "the entire labor movement in New York City" was behind the strikers. The fact is, though, that Paul Hall, president of the Seafarers International Union and a man who contributed much over the years to the development of AFSCME, was about the only labor leader of substance to support the strike meaningfully. Three union officials were fined $250 and on January 21 began serving 30 day jail sentences. Four days later 16 more union officers were sentenced to jail.

During his first day on the picket lines Wurf characterized the welfare strike in words that were to become an AFSCME theme:

> There must come a time when there is a recognition of the rights of public employees to bargain freely as equals, and without political pressures. There must come a time, too, when city and state officials understand that organized public employees seek only responsibility at the bargaining table. We think that time has come.

Though concern over wages and working conditions was implicit, Wurf emphasized equality of public employees and their desire for collective bargaining rights.

The strike ended February 1, 28 days after it started, making it the longest strike of public employees in the history of New York City. AFSCME called the strike a victory when the city agreed to the union's basic demand to include all issues submitted in the original bargaining proposal for negotiation of a new agreement. An impartial fact-finding panel consisting of labor representatives (Paul Hall and Eric Polisar) and city officials was set up to consider the issues. As AFSCME's Larry Rogin said in his chronology of unionism in public employment: "The strike initiated far-reaching changes in the city's labor relations program," changes that influenced in

158

part the later establishment of the Office of Collective Bargaining. The city also agreed to withhold any reprisals for strikers under Condon-Wadlin, and all 19 union officials were released from jail. Immediate gains were wage increases of $500 to $900 a year, reduction in workloads and increase in staff (the union maintained the staff-client ratio was too high for effective care), a 150 percent increase in the number of scholarships, a welfare fund and more group medical insurance.

Wurf: *It was a long and bitter but significant strike. We originally went out in sympathy with the radical Social Service Employees and found their people weren't much for picket lines in the dead of winter. We figured it was a setup, but we welcomed a chance to stand up to the labor-city hall alliance that we had been fighting for so long when we were trying to build a union in New York.*

I was able to take control of the strike because our local leadership up there and the leadership of the independent union had been thrown in jail. I tried to provoke the judge into putting me in jail too, but he wouldn't be provoked, which disappointed me.

Two good things came of the strike that go unnoticed. First, it was the last time we were challenged by the established powers in New York, and second, the Social Service Employees came back into our fold. After the strike they reaffiliated.

The same day the welfare strike ended, Victor Gotbaum moved from the international staff to head the 40,000-member District Council 37. He recruited Lillian Roberts, who had worked with him in Chicago, and began building a reputation for strong leadership of New York City employees. The council survived political attacks and several bitter strikes as it set the pattern for collective bargaining innovations that are still being imitated elsewhere in the country.

Late in 1965 AFSCME was again challenged, not by the New York establishment but by a relentless enemy, the Inter-

159

national Brotherhood of Teamsters, with whom there was a dispute over who would represent 34,000 hospital workers in New York City. The Teamsters had been expelled from the AFL-CIO for corruption, and George Meany came out strong for AFSCME. He sent a letter to all city hospital workers urging them to join AFSCME. An election was held December 3, pitting the Teamsters against District Council 37. Over 80 percent of the employees voted, and Council 37 scored a decisive victory, although the Teamsters contested the election and managed to hold up certification for almost a year.

Until this time AFSCME was known to very few Americans, but by 1966 the national press was taking notice of this emerging labor organization which was about to become the fastest growing international union in the country. In addition to the *Business Week* and *Life* articles, there was other significant press attention. *U.S. News and World Report* carried a long interview with Wurf, questioning him repeatedly on his outspoken stand on the right of public workers to strike. An Associated Press story distributed nationally began:

> In the first six months of this year unions hit the nation's city halls—labor's newest target—with at least thirty strikes. More are certain to follow.
>
> Nearly two-thirds of the strikes were by teachers, and the rest involved welfare workers, firemen, policemen, doctors, nurses, hospital attendants, transit workers and garbage collectors . . .
>
> There is a strong feeling on the part of employees that they've got to have something to say about wages, hours and working conditions, and civil service has not given it to them," said Robert Hastings, assistant to the president of the American Federation of State, County and Municipal Employees, largest of the national unions in the field.

160

A United Press International story read in part:

An AFL-CIO labor union is bargaining for park laborers and psychologists, policemen and workers assigned to New York's toughest "bopping gangs."

It is the fast-growing American Federation of State, County and Municipal Employees, and union president Jerry Wurf sees no paradox in his richly varied membership.

The headlines from these and other news service stories announced: "LABOR'S NEWEST TARGET—CITY HALL; GROWING MILITANCY SEEN AMONG PUBLIC EMPLOYEES; AFSCME: A UNION FOR ALMOST EVERYONE."

The reason for interest in AFSCME had much to do with the union's effectiveness that grew from the optimism and energy of the early days of the new leadership, but it was also due in part to the public's general concern over the question of public employee strikes. This concern was largely the effect of a crippling transit strike in New York City held in early 1966 by the Transport Workers Union.

The TWU was headed by Mike Quill, a born militant who had joined the labor movement in its early and violent years, a man who by remaining militant contrasted sharply with the "statesmen-like" leadership of labor's halcyon years. But Quill's militancy was also in contrast to the "new militancy" of a Wurf. As *Life* said in 1966: "What sets Wurf apart from old-style militants in his emphasis on membership involvement—'making it with the little guy,' he puts it. 'I don't want to control any members,' he explains, 'I want to involve them.' He also involves himself at every level . . ."

Quill's biographer, L. H. Whittemore, explains in his book, *The Man Who Ran the Subways,* that Quill's success with his membership and the employer—usually the city of New York—was the result of a contrived method which combined public abuse of city officials and private negotiations with the same officials and an eleventh hour settlement, made

161

all the more dramatic by the fact that TWU contracts always expired at the stroke of midnight on New Year's Eve.

For years Quill threatened a New Year transit strike and for years managed to get a settlement, but in January 1966 the scheme went awry, and Quill was caught amidst his membership, the retiring mayor, Robert Wagner, and the incoming mayor, John Lindsay, who did not understand Quill's method, believed the press when it accused Quill of his usual bluff and stood firmly against any wage increase Quill could take back to his rank and file. Quill, beleaguered and ill, realized he was left with no choice, so he struck.

The result was exactly as bad as every newspaper had been predicting every two years. The city was paralyzed by its traffic. Lindsay issued a plea to New Yorkers: "Please, if you're not essential to your job, remain at home. Now I know that every man, when he's shaving in the morning, likes to think of himself as essential. But remember there are degrees of essentiality."

Whittemore described the situation:

In most other cities, a transit strike barely can be tolerated, but in New York the dependence upon public transportation is critical. When Quill halted the subways and buses he triggered a near collapse of the city's ability to function. Cars backed up on the highways almost all the way to the suburbs from which they had come. Railroad terminals were so jammed that commuters, if they managed to get into the city at all, were forced to wait hours to get standing room on an outbound train. Many people, following Lindsay's example, walked over bridges and for dozens of blocks to get to work. To make things worse, a biting wind and rain marred the scenery and their dispositions. Low-income workers—those who could least afford to lose a day's pay—were unable to commute from one side

162

of New York to the other. As the days wore on, stores, corporations and other economic institutions, as well as schools and public services, were unable to function adequately.

Merchants flooded the New York offices of the Small Business Administration with requests for survival loans, welfare roles swelled and businesses throughout the nation lost vast amounts of money because of their dependence on New York's freight transportation. Lindsay was finally forced to settle on terms quite favorable to the union, although Quill was able to enjoy the victory for only two days. He died of heart failure on January 28.

AFSCME had supported the strike in a carefully worded editorial in the January 1966 issue of *The Public Employee:*

Let the record show that while we regret that the Transport Workers Union was forced to go on strike we consider they had a legitimate grievance.

We are naturally concerned about the fact that eight million New Yorkers, including many thousands of our members, were left without transportation when the buses and subways were struck. We regret the imposition of hardship upon the many small merchants who have had to turn to the Small Business Administration for loans to tide them over the grim days when business was virtually at a standstill.

Thousands upon thousands of words were written about the rigors of living in a great city without the benefit of mass transportation. But in all of the published reports on the strike's progress and its attendant hardships, there was no adequate explanation of the fact that the transport workers were not receiving pay on a parity with other New York City workers. Their pay was not on a par with mem-

163

bers of our union, nor with that of persons doing similar work.

We are happy that, according to published reports, the workers got a break when the settlement was finally reached.

Yes, there were hardships for New Yorkers as a result of the strike. But do not let all of the newspaper reports of these hardships obscure the fact that the members of the Transport Workers Union had a legitimate grievance.

The AFSCME editorialist apparently felt that events often get exaggerated exposure simply by occurring in New York. The TWU was a national union, the argument continues, and it had gone out on strike in other cities—most notably Philadelphia—without nearly so much notoriety. But the New York strike invited a wave of editorials, attacks by politicians and the creation of study commissions. As the spotlight focused on the New York transit strike, the growing militancy of public workers became a national issue.

On the other hand, it is highly probable that public employee unionism would have received attention in the midsixties, New York transit strike or no strike. In *Public Workers and Public Unions* Arnold M. Zack lists eight underlying reasons why:

- An expanding demand for public service that brought about a dramatic increase in public employment without an increase in wages, creating a lag between public sector and industrial wages.
- Public employees questioning their exclusion from the rights and protection afforded private employees by the National Labor Relations Act.
- An influx of younger, more militant and more largely male personnel who sought to mobilize the public sector to seek greater benefits.

164

- The granting of prevailing wages to construction workers working for the government under Davis-Bacon and similar laws, which prompted other government workers to try to match those wages.
- Attempts by trade unions in the private sector to begin organizing state and local employees to fill their declining membership and the stimulating effect of those attempts on previously passive organizations like the National Education Association.
- A broad interpretation of President Kennedy's Executive Order 10988.
- The demonstrated power of rising civil disobedience in the civil rights and draft resister movements, anti-poverty campaigns and war protests, which convinced militant public employees of the viability of protesting against the "establishment" to bring about change.
- And ". . . most importantly, the demonstrated success of initial illegal strikes such as the New York transit strike and some of the early teachers' strikes became powerful proof that the *power* to strike was of far greater relevance than the *right* to strike. As long as some employees obtained improvements from the strikes, others recognized it as a useful vehicle for their protest as well."

Zack refers to the issue that was central to the colloquy between Wirtz and Wurf at the 1966 AFSCME convention. He notes the importance of the transit strike and makes a necessary distinction between the power to strike and the right to strike. AFSCME had learned the importance of that power in the 1965 welfare workers' strike, which was one of the big, "illegal" public employee strikes that proved the impotence of the Condon-Wadlin approach to labor relations in government.

1966 was a year of growing militancy. A strike in Durham, N.C. early in the year was disappointing, but two day walkouts by city employees in Toledo, Youngstown and Dayton, Ohio were much more effective. A longer strike in Lansing, Michigan was successful, and an eight day walkout in Warren, Ohio even more so. When a group of unorganized county sanitation employees in Maryland walked off their jobs, AFSCME rushed to the scene, got the group's permission to represent them and negotiated a successful agreement.

In July 1966 AFSCME got an important collective bargaining law passed in the state of Wisconsin. A month later at a meeting of its executive board AFSCME passed a resolution affirming the right of public employees, law enforcement officers excepted, to strike, a resolution that was endorsed by the 1968 AFSCME convention. And in September 1966 the 34,000 New York hospital workers who had voted to join District Council 37 were certified and by December had received annual pay increases of $900 to $1500.

Strike activity continued into 1967. In January welfare workers returned to their jobs in Cleveland after winning a 15 day strike; in February sanitation workers in York, Pennsylvania received a sizable pay raise after a walkout of four weeks, and an 11 day strike by unorganized workers at the University of Ohio resulted in agreement to every demand, including full representation by AFSCME. In Philadelphia, to stop the city's foot dragging on a pension plan virtually all the city employees took a one day AFSCME sponsored holiday and got their pension.

While all this successful strike activity continued, publicity surrounding the early strikes in New York City—especially the transit strike—was having an adverse effect. Encouraged by that publicity and public reaction and realizing that state and local governments across the country were watching, New York Governor Nelson Rockefeller maneuvered a bill through the State Legislature, the purpose of which was to control public worker unionism. It was passed in April 1967, replacing the Condon-Wadlin Act of 1947. Adopting the name of its co-sponsors, labor called it the Rocky-Travia Act (Rockefeller-Travia), more widely known as the Taylor law, after the late George W. Taylor, a University of Pennsylvania professor who headed a commission that proposed the law. Condon-Wadlin had been considered by organized labor to be one of the most repressive public employee laws ever passed, but it had one advantage from labor's standpoint—it was virtually unenforceable. In 20 years Condon-Wadlin had been invoked only eight times (the last time against AFSCME's welfare workers' strike in New York in 1965).

The new law guaranteed unions the right to organize and bargain for New York's state, county and municipal employees, set up a Public Employment Relations Board to resolve representational disputes and provide mediation and fact finding help and required state and all political subdivisions to bargain collectively with public employees.

On the other hand it barred strikes and set heavy penalties for strikers, unions and union leaders. It stipulated fines of $10,000 or a week's dues, whichever would be less, per strike day, and a union could lose its dues checkoff for as much as 18 months. Striking workers could be fired. Worst of all, the law appeared enforceable.

On May 23, 1967, AFSCME District Council 37, the Transport Workers Union and the United Teachers Federation, backed by their internationals, staged a 25,000 member rally in Madison Square Garden to protest the Rocky-Travia Act. Paul Hall, president of the Seafarers International Union, told the crowd the act was "reprehensible to the very spirit of free trade unionism," and Wurf called it "the rat law."

Following the welfare strike in 1966, the city had set up a tripartite panel—with Victor Gotbaum, executive director of District Council 37 as a member—to study and make recom-

167

mendations on labor problems in the city. The study resulted in the formation of the Office of Collective Bargaining, a seven member body composed of two city officials, two labor representatives and four impartial members. The first of its kind in the country, OCB was hailed by Wurf as the "model for collective bargaining in the public service," marking an end to employer domination in public service-management relations. OCB provided specific procedures for achieving certification as a bargaining representative, negotiating contracts, processing grievances, mediation, fact-finding and arbitration in impasse situations.

1968 opened with the Teamsters Union taking the New York City sanitation workers out on strike on February 7, 1968.

As with the transit strike the action swiftly escalated into a crisis. In the exaggerated way in which things often happen in New York nearly 100,000 tons of garbage piled up within a week. The garbage was rat infested and fire prone, and public health authorities, warning of typhoid and other diseases, proclaimed the city's first general health emergency since the 1931 polio epidemic.

Mayor Lindsay, whose rivalry with fellow Republican Gov. Nelson Rockefeller was intense at the time, declared the garbage workers' strike to be in violation of the Taylor Law and called on the governor to send in National Guard troops to pick up the garbage. But Teamsters President John DeLury had supported Rockefeller when the governor pressured the legislature into adopting the Taylor Law, and the governor resisted sending in troops to thwart his labor supporter's strike against the city.

By the end of 1968 Lindsay had experienced several more public worker crises. Police called in sick, firemen refused to answer routine calls and the city's teachers staged several lockouts and a strike. Press coverage became more and more critical as the year wore on.

Public workers were going on strike across the country,

but the big walkouts in New York got the most attention. As Whittemore suggested, the city's size explained much of it, for in spite of—or perhaps as a result of—the strike activities, New York was by and large far ahead in its relations with its employees. Most public workers in New York were more familiar with traditional trade unionism, and those who had joined a public employee union for the first time were beginning to get experience with collective bargaining procedures.

The issues surrounding the strikes could be directly connected with the special problems of public worker-civic employer relations: the right to strike, extent to which certain unions represented working groups and the right of bilateral appeal for impartial judgment.

Even though strikes usually concern wages in one way or another, Wurf in a *U.S. News and World Report* interview wasn't sure that is always the case with the AFSCME member:

> I think, when one talks about the strike in a public service, one has to bear in mind certain important facts: To begin with, public employees traditionally are not precipitous people. They're not people who look for a strike.
>
> The reason our people strike may not be closely tied to wage problems, as might be the case in the private sector. However, wages might be a factor.
>
> I remember a strike I was involved in about a year and a half ago where the employer, at every meeting kept handing us a copy of a state statute telling us we had practically no rights and, therefore, he wouldn't settle the grievance. Our people went out on strike in sheer indignation at the fact that the employer wouldn't responsibly deal with his condition of employment.

Hospital workers of AFSCME District Council 37, New York City, vote to approve a contract

9.   A Strike for Recognition as a Man

*This is not New York and nothing will be gained
by ignoring our laws . . . I intend to do my duty
since this work involves the public health.*

Henry Loeb, III, mayor of Memphis,
Tennessee, February 12, 1968

On Wednesday, January 31, 1968, a month after Henry
Loeb had been sworn in as mayor, it rained in Memphis, Tennessee. Twenty-two employees of the Sewer and Drain Main-
tenance Division of the Department of Public Works were
sent home because of the rain. All of them were black. White
employees with identical work classifications remained on the
job and received a full day's wages.

The city offered to pay the workers two hours callup pay
when it received complaints from the blacks, but it was not
enough to appease the workers, who, backed by Local 1733,
AFSCME, were concerned as much about the racism of the act
as about the money.

Other things bothered the group as well. The day after
the rainstorm two sanitation workers were killed in an accident on a city truck. The deaths dramatized the problems
many blacks thought characterized their employment by the
city—inadequate safety controls, no medical protection or
other common benefits.

The two incidents and growing disaffection of the

workers led T. O. Jones, president of Local 1733, to call a meeting of the union and to plan a work stoppage for Monday, February 12.

A last minute attempt was made by both the mayor's office and Jones to resolve the workers' grievances. After two and a half hours of discussion failed to produce any kind of satisfactory agreement, Jones told the mayor, "Call up the chancellor and tell him to lock me up. I'm going out on strike." Jones opened a paper sack he had brought to the meeting, took out a set of old, worn clothes and changed into them. Mayor Loeb asked "What's that?" and Jones replied, "These are my going-to-jail clothes."

On Monday morning all but 200 of the 1,300 workers walked off their jobs. Only 38 of the city's 180 garbage trucks made pickups, and trash began to pile up in Memphis at the rate of 2,600 tons a day.

It began as a minor strike with racial overtones. Headlines announced that Mayor Loeb hoped for an early settlement. AFSCME officials in Washington didn't find out about plans for the strike until the weekend before it took place, when a Memphis newspaperman called headquarters to get comments. But by the time the sanitation men had walked off their jobs early on the morning of Feb. 12, AFSCME was foursquare in support of the strike and had dispatched international staff officials P.J. Ciampa, William Lucy, Jesse Epps and Joe Paisley to Memphis. Wurf himself arrived there February 18, and he was to remain until the strike was settled, returning to Washington for brief visits to attend to urgent business or see his wife, Mildred, who was pregnant.

If Loeb had really envisioned an early end to the strike, he did not demonstrate a knowledge of how to achieve that goal. On Tuesday an AFSCME field director, Ciampa, had flown in from Washington to meet with the mayor. They had exchanged harsh words, and Ciampa ended the meeting by calling Loeb a liar and a dictator. Then on Wednesday, in answer to a challenge Loeb had hurled at the union leadership

172

that they did not truly represent the city's employees, over 1,000 strikers marched on city hall. Led by Jones, the workers sat in Ellis Auditorium until the mayor came to face them.

Loeb has been described as a "hard-driving, self-initiative, shirtsleeves politician." He was born in Memphis of an old line Jewish family and educated at Phillips Andover Academy and Brown University. He commanded a PT boat in the Mediterranean during World War II. First elected to office as public works commissioner for the city in 1956, he became mayor of Memphis in 1960 but resigned to take over the family laundry business when his father died in 1964. When he was reelected to the mayor's office in 1968 with virtually no support from the black community, he came in under a new form of city government, the mayor-council system, approved by voters in a 1966 referendum.

On the other side was Local 1733, a predominantly black union. Its president, Jones, had been fired by the city for an organizing effort in 1963. From the time it received its charter from AFSCME in October 1964, 1733 had sought unsuccessfully to gain recognition from the city. Commissioner T. E. Sisson, elected public works commissioner in 1963, had promised the union recognition in exchange for political support, but once in office he denied the offer, contending the city was prevented by law from negotiating with a union. A planned strike for recognition in 1965 was poorly organized, and word of it leaked to city officials who obtained an injunction against the potential strikers before the walkout began. Added to the lack of organization had been the presence at that time of a mayor, William Ingram, whose popularity with the black community—despite serious doubts as to the sincerity of his interest in workers' and blacks' problems—made it difficult to gather support from either members of the local or the black community at large. Generally aggravating the whole problem in the struggle for recognition was the old commission form of government, which allowed the commissioners to avoid the question by hiding behind one another.

173

But the new mayor under the new system was not afforded that luxury. The question of recognition became the sole responsibility of his office. "This was fine," noted Dan Powell, southeastern regional director of the AFL-CIO's Committee on Political Education, "except the wrong man was elected to office."

What the union demanded of the "wrong man" at Ellis Auditorium that first Wednesday of the strike was a pay raise, recognition of AFSCME as its sole bargaining agent, dues checkoff, seniority rights, a merit promotion system, health and hospital insurance, safety controls and a meaningful grievance procedure. (The average sanitation laborer in Memphis was making $3,744 yearly. A 33 percent wage increase would have raised that salary to $4,992.)

Loeb would not listen. He took the position that the strike was illegal and there could be no negotiations whatsoever until the strikers returned to their jobs. The "law" the mayor invoked was the same "law" Sisson had cited in 1963 and the same "law" the Tennessee state court judge had used in the injunction against the aborted strike of 1965. The "law" was actually a decision handed down in two separate cases by the Tennessee Supreme Court which held that strikes against the public were illegal. The judge issuing the injunction against the 1965 strike had expanded the decision to include picketing against the city as well. However, there was no law and there never had been a Supreme Court decision on the legality of forming a public workers union nor on recognition and negotiation with such a union. All that was covered by the various decisions were actual strike activities.

On the surface neither the union's demands nor the mayor's original stand were that unusual. True, Memphis had never experienced an extended public workers' strike, but it certainly had heard of them. In 1968 no one could ignore the growing occurrence of such strikes. From the time Mike Quill had led his transit workers off the job in New York City in 1966 up to the time of New York City's sanitation strike by the

174

Teamster's union, public workers' strikes had been national news. But Loeb was fond of claiming in a confrontation, "This is not New York."

Had it been a question of basic union demands and the mayor's first response to them, the early settlement Loeb hoped for might have become a reality. One side might have compromised a little; mediators might have been consulted rather than dismissed out of hand; perhaps at the most arbitration might have been considered. Instead, the race issue became central. "I *am* a man," was the workers' slogan, for recognition of the union became the same for blacks as their recognition as human beings. New to the job and saddled with an untested form of government and a city council that was weak and unsure of itself, Loeb, a white mayor of a city whose 700,000 population was 40 percent black, did not understand the meaning of that slogan.

He did not understand even after the black community in Memphis, traditionally splintered among various political factions and religious groups, rallied behind the slogan. He did not understand later when national figures like Roy Wilkins, Bayard Rustin and Martin Luther King came to marches and demonstrations in support of the strike, nor when top level leadership from the AFSCME international— including Jerry Wurf—began to take an active part in the local's activity.

Loeb tried to emphasize that it was a union dispute, a question of employer-employee relationships, of legality in the strictest sense, even after the riots and the "outside agitators" and his own obstinancy began to point to something larger than Memphis, something symbolic, something even more familiar to the country and certainly to the south than public workers' strikes.

Not understanding, Mayor Loeb told the thousand-odd black workers gathered in Ellis Auditorium for the first round of a long fight that the trash would be picked up in Memphis. That was his only problem, his only concern. He issued the

175

strikers an ultimatum. They could either be on the job by 7 a.m. the next morning, or he would hire someone else to pick up the trash. He told them: "Bet on it." The speed with which the strike grew to a full-fledged black-white confrontation and the size to which it grew surprised even AFSCME officials. As Jesse Epps, a key black staff member of AFSCME who worked closely with the strikers from the second day of the strike, admitted later, not only did the union "not think it would escalate as it did," but it also did not see the strike as having much impact on the union's southern organization until almost two weeks into the affair when the city's position began to harden beyond compromise and forced the black community together.

Memphis, unlike other southern cities of its size during the '60s, was thought to be fairly moderate in its treatment of its black minority and to enjoy a certain racial tranquility. Desegregation of its schools began in October 1961, though by 1968 over 80 percent of black children in Memphis still attended predominantly black schools. The relatively early beginning and slow followup were emblematic. Change was on the surface, and though by southern standards it could not be called token, there existed problems of job discrimination in upgrading and promotion and exclusion from supervisory positions. The problems extended to housing as well and, most importantly of all, to police-community relations.

To be fair, Loeb was probably as much a victim of this image of Memphis as anyone. He had been described as a man who wanted to be fair but whose idea of equity came out of white middle-class society. His adamant stand against union recognition was apparently less a race question than anti-union bias. One thing he did understand clearly was that to recognize the union was to change the structure of city government radically. Yet by not doing so he effectively kept blacks out of the decision-making processes of the city, denying them the right to influence their own destiny.

His misjudgment in handling the police is probably the

clearest indication of his inability to grasp the total problem. The black community was particularly incensed at such injustices by the Memphis police department as were reported by the 1966 Civil Rights Commission hearings which warned: "Relations between the police and the Negro community are in a sad state of disrepair. Only prompt, bold and decisive leadership on the part of the highest officials of the city and county can avert the disaster which may coincide with the next incident." Under those conditions, to bring the police out in large numbers as a show of force and to turn them loose on strikers in an early march, as Loeb did, was more than a tactical error.

True to his word Loeb hired a few men to make selected trash pickups on February 15, the morning following his ultimatum, and the trucks were given a police escort. On February 16 the local NAACP endorsed the strike and in the next few days held an all night vigil and proposed a boycott of downtown stores. On Sunday, February 18, Wurf arrived with a $5,000 check for Local 1733 and attended an all night meeting with the mayor arranged by a group of white ministers mainly interested in a quick settlement. Then on Thursday, February 22, more than 1,000 sanitation workers and supporters staged a rowdy sit-in at a Public Works Committee hearing, and the committee passed a resolution to be read to the City Council the following day calling for recognition of the union and a form of dues checkoff. When it was read at their meeting on Friday, February 23, the City Council passed a sutstitute resolution which accepted all the demands *but* recognition and dues checkoff. The council refused to hear from citizens and strikers sitting in on the meeting. In response the strikers broke up the meeting and staged their first march down Main Street. The police moved in and forcefully broke up the march.

The police used a chemical called mace and their nightsticks, although no car had actually been overturned, no windows broken, no stores looted. The brutality was followed

177

by swift legal actions by the city. On Saturday, February 24, an injunction was obtained against striking and picketing.

The most important result, however, was the effect the violence had on the black ministers in Memphis. As Dr. Ralph Jackson, director of the Deparment of Mimimum Salary of the African Methodist Episcopal Church and an active spokesman for the black community during the strike, described it to a meeting of strikers and the black community: "I have a confession to make. For 30 years I have been training to hold myself in check. I couldn't understand what made some people lose control of themselves and fly off the handle. I never thought it could happen to me. But I lost 30 years of training in just five minutes last Friday."

The black ministers of Memphis did not have a record of standing up to the white establishment, but they ruled the black community through a group of what has been called "little fiefdoms." The ministers had not always been unified, but the incidents of February 22-23 caused them to form an organization called the Committee on the Move for Equality (COME), an organization that was able to call an effective boycott of downtown stores when it was rebuffed by the City Council. Within a week downtown merchants reported a 25 percent drop in sales. It was this organization that was able to deliver large numbers of demonstrators from the entire black community to support the daily marches downtown, beginning February 26, that were to continue throughout the entire strike. It was this organization to which the city felt it necessary to turn to control the increasing militancy of younger blacks. It was this group who helped engineer the breaking of the local news "freeze" on the strike. And it was a leader, Rev. James Lawson, who got Dr. Martin Luther King, Jr. to come to Memphis.

When King arrived in Memphis the first time on March 18, 1968, the strike was 36 days old. A number of important events had occurred to increase the intensity of the strike:

178

- Loeb had proposed a compromise settlement which had been seriously considered by the union, but he then backed down.
- 23 union members, including Wurf, had been cited for contempt.
- A riot bill had been passed by the state legislature.
- Loeb had sent each striker an individual letter inviting him back to work.
- Two union supporters were arrested for jaywalking.
- Loeb's family businesses had had their windows smashed.
- The strikers had received their first open support from organized labor when 500 white union members from Memphis marched with the strikers.
- Black power pamphlets had begun to appear.
- 116 demonstrators were arrested for a sit-in at city hall.
- On March 6 strikers had held a mock funeral for freedom at City Hall.
- There had been trouble at Le Moyne College over the word "niggra."
- Both Bayard Rustin and Roy Wilkins had spoken to mass rallies in Memphis.
- On the day King arrived in Memphis, 3,000 national guardsmen at Loeb's request held riot drills after they had bivouacked within the city limits.

When Lawson first contacted him at the end of February, King had been reluctant to come to Memphis. He was in the midst of organizing his poor people's campaign which was to culminate in a march from Montgomery to Washington. In December 1967 he had first announced the plans for what he hoped would be the largest non-violent demonstration in the nation's history, and since that time things had not gone well for planning the march.

Memphis seemed an interruption, but King came. Gerald Frank has suggested in his book, *An American Death,* that the reason King came was that he saw in the strike a microcosm of the poor people's campaign itself:

> The trouble in Memphis had been brewing for years. To the black garbage and sewer workers it seemed that all the disabilities of the Negro were concentrated in their lot. In a city known for its low wages, they had one of the lowest paying jobs, and one scorned by everyone else. There was no job security, no insurance. The leather tubs in which they hauled the garbage on their shoulders were old and leaking, causing painful skin blisters. Warned not to lunch in cafés lest they drink beer and become intoxicated, the men ate in the street. They had no facilities for either washing or personal comfort, and if they used a field or ravine, white residents made outraged calls to the police. Whites also objected if they took refuge from Memphis torrential rains on their porches. They had a specified number of streets to complete in their seven-to-three-o'clock day, and if they were eight or ten houses short by quitting time, they had to continue work without overtime pay or be docked.

As early as 1961 King had called for a coalition of labor and the civil rights movement. The AFSCME local with its almost total black membership as well as the size of black membership in the international union were a good beginning for such a coalition.

Martin Luther King arrived back in Memphis March 18 and was well received at a rally of 17,000 strikers and supporters. He said he was going back to Montgomery to com-

Sanitation workers' signs articulate true issue of Memphis strike

plete arrangements for the Poor People's March, and he called for a citywide demonstration on his return the following Friday, March 22.

King's return and the mass march were postponed when a record breaking snowstorm prevented King's plane from leaving Montgomery. The march was rescheduled for Thursday, March 28. It was supposed to be another example of the power of non-violent civil disobedience, but something was to go wrong. Events preceding the march did not bode well. For example, on March 23 mediation sessions between the city and AFSCME officials began, but ended in failure on March 27, the evening before King returned, when union officials walked out after they were told by city representatives, "We are not authorized to agree on any issue but only to discuss issues." Earlier that day Loeb had told a Lions club meeting that he would not budge from his hardline position.

Thus on March 28 there was an atmosphere of general frustration at yet another failed attempt to get the city to deal with the strikers. On top of this, demonstrators who had gathered at Clayborn Temple for the march that was to begin at 9 a.m. were faced with the specific frustration of waiting several hours for the arrival of King. They were told by loud-speaker that his plane would land about 10:30, and the march could begin shortly afterward.

King did not arrive at the temple until almost eleven, and the march lurched forward at 11:05. Meanwhile the waiting demonstrators heard a rumor that police had used clubs and mace to prevent a group of high school students from leaving school to join the march. A 14 year old girl was said to have been hospitalized with head lacerations. Confused reports of this and other incidents ran through the crowd, causing concern, increasing tension.

The mounting tension was reflected in other ways. Pleas of leaders to clear the sidewalks and ground around the church and to take places at the rear of the line were ignored. Not far from Clayborn Temple 25 men raided a liquor store.

The signs carried by the demonstrators read "I AM A MAN",
the strike's slogan, and many others ironically proclaimed
LOEB FOR GOD, but youths who had refused to join the
march and had gathered at street corners wrote their own epi-
grams. DAMN LOEB—BLACK POWER IS HERE, LOVE MY ASS.
Others described the mayor in even more obscene language.

The march began. As it turned left on Beale Street
headed toward Main, the demonstrators passed through
crowds of spectators. Then within two blocks of Main there
came the crack and tingle of shattering glass. Demonstrators
could see a youth in his late teens smash a window on one side
of the street, then move along behind the spectators up the
other side, whacking out windows with a club, one after the
other.

As the march turned onto Main, the window breaking
continued, and it was not sporadic or isolated vandalism.
Policemen, wearing gas masks and carrying riot gear, blocked
Main Street. The adjoining streets were filled with demonstrators, the sidewalks with spectators. King was forced by his
aides to leave the march and return to his motel. Lawson got a
loudspeaker, identified himself and asked the marchers to go
back to the temple. The crowd began to break up. Ten
minutes later the police made their move and headed for the
intersection of Main and Beale. They were greeted with picket
signs and other missiles thrown by youths. Tear gas grenades
exploded, crowds of young blacks ran down Beale Street in
retreat, and the violence began.

When it was over, 280 people had been arrested, 60
(mostly blacks) injured, fires set, property damaged, stores
looted, the National Guard called out, a curfew ordered and a
16 year old black youth killed by police gunfire.

The next day newspapers all over the country carried
accounts of the march, the death of Larry Payne and accusations against King. Instead of proving once again the viability
of non-violence, Memphis had showed its failure. King
defended himself by explaining that he and his staff had not

been involved in planning the Memphis march and were not aware of the potential for violence.

King was not the only one concerned with the militancy of some Memphis blacks. The ministers who were leading the community in support of the strike were concerned for the safety of their people and uneasy over fringe groups outside their control, but they were not beyond using that element as coercion against the city. The city, for its part, was using strikebreakers, a show of police force and the National Guard to put pressure on the strikers.

King's call for a civil rights-labor coalition impressed Wurf. While black separatism in the north might be possible, in the south it could only do damage, for effective opposition was hampered by lack of institutional muscle with which to fight the establishment. In fact, southern whites had made separatism their civic dogma because it was the best arrangement for keeping have-nots in their place. So the primary goal of the strike became union recognition and not the wage increase. Perhaps that is also why it became the one thing on which Loeb would not back down. And it was why the strikers' slogan, "I *am* a man", became the slogan of the entire black community.

Wurf had first come down to Memphis on February 18 at the insistence of some members of his staff without truly realizing the problems involved in a strike by southern blacks. He learned quickly. He faced Loeb and met a brick wall. He marched into the early police brutality. He was arrested, fined and sentenced to jail for contempt.

On Friday, March 29, the day after the rally had erupted into violence, 300 sanitation workers and ministers made a peaceful and silent march from Clayborn Temple to City Hall. They were followed by five armored personnel carriers, five jeeps, three military trucks and dozens of National Guardsmen with fixed bayonets. That same day Mayor Loeb turned down an offer of assistance in mediating the affair from President Lyndon Johnson and AFL-CIO President George Meany.

The events of those two days led King to call off a trip to Africa and to announce he would return to Memphis to lead a peaceful march.

On April 2 funeral services were held for Larry Payne. He was not the first black youth killed in Memphis during the strike. Earlier a sniper shot a six year old, but that time the killer did not wear a uniform. Payne's funeral was attended by hundreds of blacks and was featured prominently in national and local news. A photograph of Payne's mother crying over his coffin must have moved King and others deeply.

The day before Larry Payne's funeral Loeb had decided things were settled enough for him to lift the curfew, and on the day of the funeral the National Guard was withdrawn. But the atmosphere in Memphis was still tense.

On April 3, Dr. King returned. He addressed a huge rally at Mason Temple that night. In his speech he talked of assassination. He recounted the story of an attempted assassination in New York in 1958. "Like anybody I would like to live; longevity has its place. But I'm not concerned about that now. I just want to do God's will. And He's allowed me to go up to the mountain. And I've looked over and I've seen the Promised Land. I may not get there with you, but I want you to know, tonight, that we as a people will get to the Promised Land. So I'm happy tonight. I'm not worried about anything. I'm not fearing any man. Mine eyes have seen the glory of the coming of the Lord."

That same morning, April 3, a Tennessee judge had issued a temporary restraining order against the march. King had labelled the order a basic denial of the First Amendment, but despite it the march was scheduled to take place on time. It was to be a big march with as many as 6,000 supporters coming from all over the country. Bayard Rustin had suggested to King that he make the march a major, nonviolent demonstration, hoping that outstanding union leaders would take part.

The planning sessions took up the better part of the next

day, April 4. A few minutes before 6:00 p.m., Martin Luther King stepped out onto his balcony. He leaned over the railing to talk to Jesse Jackson and another man below in the courtyard. As he did so, a white man watching him from across the way shot him. The bullet entered the back of Martin Luther King's neck and came out his jaw. Martin Luther King was dead.

The rioting that tore cities apart across the nation in the aftermath of King's assassination did not strike Memphis with the same force and destructiveness as elsewhere. The black ministers asserted their control, and relatively little damage was done. On April 8 a memorial march was held in Memphis in honor of King, led by Coretta King and Ralph Abernathy. Jerry Wurf was in the front line of marchers, along with Walter Reuther. On April 9 King was buried in Atlanta, Georgia.

On April 5 Undersecretary of Labor James Reynolds arrived to serve as a mediator of the strike, sent by President Johnson. From the beginning mediation in one form or another had been going on sporadically or had been offered. As early as March 4 State Sen. Frank White had proposed a bill to create a non-binding mediation board to resolve the impasse, but the mayor had opposed it. Informal talks started by various citizens' groups had started and stopped. As late as April 4, for example, two hours before the assassination, 15 top businessmen in Memphis had met with Tom Powell, Memphis labor council president, and come up with an offer of $25,000 to pay the strikers' union dues if they would go back to work. Wurf said of the offer: ". . . [it's] more than outrageous, it's laughable." On March 23 official non-binding mediation sessions had begun with Frank Miles, an experienced Memphis mediator, but he had suspended the talks until further notice on March 27 when the union walked out of the meetings.

Part of the mediation problem came from real ignorance of labor disputes on Loeb's part. According to Miles, Loeb did not at first understand the distinction between mediation, a method of defining issues in a dispute, and arbitration, an effort to reach a compromise on the issues, and the terms had to be clarified again and again. Loeb constantly referred to the strikers as "his" men and kept reminding the mediators that as a former public works commissioner he understood the problems of the workers better than the union leadership. This attitude was crucial because it seriously blocked any settlement when black workers began to focus their stand on the issue of recognition.

The pressures on Loeb were mounting. AFL-CIO councils all over the country were raising money and publicly pledging support to the strikers. George Meany set up a special national fund for the strike, giving Local 1733 an initial $20,000. The United Auto Workers donated $50,000. Memphians—especially the business community—began to react to the publicity and, fearing the image the nation was getting of their city, urged Loeb to reach a settlement. The man who had gone so far as to cut off food stamps for strikers now had no choice but to negotiate.

Even after Reynolds arrived, however, negotiations did not go smoothly. He had his first meeting with Loeb on April 6. It was the start of a long series of meetings, first with one side, then the other, meetings which finally ended on April 16. Toward the end Loeb was insisting the city had no funds to provide workers with a raise, and subsequently the union's demand was lowered. Settlement came after a threat by Ralph Abernathy on April 15 that unless the strike were settled in two days, he would stage another mass march on City Hall. The day before the settlement both the boycott of downtown merchants and the picketing increased considerably.

In light of the city's consistent hardline refusals, the terms of the settlement constituted a clear victory for AFSCME, though Loeb insisted, "This is not a victory for anyone except the entire community." The settlement included a 10 cent raise beginning May 1, 1968 and another 5 cent raise on September 1; non-exclusive union recognition of AFSCME (but recognition of AFSCME as the sole representative of laborers, truck drivers and crew chiefs of the sanitation department, in other words, of the membership of Local 1733); a clause on anti-racial discrimination in hiring and promotion; promotions based on seniority and competence; a meaningful grievance procedure; dues checkoff; a no-strike clause during the time period covered by the contract; and a clause on no discrimination against the strikers. The strike had lasted 65 days when it ended April 16.

On April 18, 40 hospital employees organized by AFSCME in Memphis walked off the job. If the first strike settlement could be called a victory for the union, the settlement involving the hospital workers, which was reached very quickly, could only be called disappointing. No wage increase was granted, but dues checkoff through a credit union was approved. Perhaps the strikes were too close. Though the elements were potentially the same, the energy was just not there in the community.

Not long after the end of the Memphis sanitation strike Wurf made plans to organize the south city by city in an ambitious drive, but it never transpired. For one thing, 1968 was a year of national trauma; the King assassination was followed in two months by the murder of Robert Kennedy in California, during his campaign for the presidency.

There was a sanitation strike in St. Petersburg, Florida in the summer of '68 and a hospital workers strike in Charleston, South Carolina in '69. They were fairly successful but were not AFSCME actions. In Huntsville, Alabama in '71 there was an AFSCME strike, but it was broken by the city. In the words of one official of the union who did time in the Huntsville jail: "There was just not the kind of national concern to help support the strike that had existed in 1968."

Bill Lucy Remembers Memphis

(Bill Lucy, a native of Memphis and one of the labor

188

movement's top black leaders, is secretary-treasurer of AFSCME. As an international staff official in 1968 he was assigned under a trusteeship to direct Council 77 in Detroit.)

I got a call from Jerry who told me to get right down to Memphis and meet P.J. Ciampa there. I had heard about the possibility of a strike but didn't think it would amount to much. I left my car in an airport parking lot and flew south.

I got a rundown from T.O. Jones on the grievances, and the real problem seemed to be that we needed somebody, some reasonably sympathetic city official, who would sit down and talk about the situation.

They had made a decision to strike by the time we met on Monday night, but the question remained how effective that decision would be. When I arrived at the sanitation yard early Tuesday morning, it was clear nobody was going in. There were a lot of guys milling around, wondering what to do, though it was obvious they had decided to support the strike.

I went to work with Ciampa, Jesse Epps and Joe Paisley, another international staffer who had come in from Tennessee, making a list of the workers' concerns and trying to find somebody to meet with. We advised the men not to go to work but not to picket the truck yard. Since nobody was going in, there was no need to picket the property.

There were a number of issues. Safety was one. A couple of guys had been killed on the job, and the union advised the city some of its equipment wasn't safe. But the straw that broke the camel's back was sending the black crews home on a day it rained and not paying them, while white crews were allowed to work and get paid for a full day. That was the issue that sparked the walkout.

We were finally able to get a meeting in Loeb's office, and we presented our beef about the grievance procedure. The mayor had absolutely no understanding of the gravity of the thing, and he took a typical city father's position: there really was no problem, the union was only trying to manufacture one and if the union would only step out of the picture, he and the men could resolve their differences easily. We went around

189

and around, but nothing was accomplished other than that we got to know the mayor and he got to know us.

A rubber workers local let us use their meeting hall, so on Wednesday we assembled the men, as we would every day from then on, to report on the lack of progress in the meeting with the mayor. That afternoon we went back to see Loeb, and the only headway I could feel we made was to hear the mayor tell us benignly that his door was always open.

Thursday was the day each week when the mayor held open house, inviting anyone to come in and present his problem. So we said at our noon meeting that since it was open house day, let's everybody go down and talk to the mayor. That meant a thousand men, and we walked to city hall, so that was the first march of the strike, and it was very noticeable.

Only a few of us could actually go inside the mayor's office, but we told him we'd brought some of the men with us and suggested he look out the window. He was obviously shocked at the size of the crowd, but he tried to show he was keeping control of the situation. He was sure that if he could speak to the men, he could show them the error of their ways and the bad direction we were giving them. He agreed to open Ellis Auditorium for a meeting right then and there.

The ground rules were that he would address the men, then I would have my chance, and whoever won their loyalty, that was it. I was practicing a little demagogy that I don't believe Loeb understood. We filed the men into the hall, told them the mayor wanted to talk with them and he was entitled to be treated with courtesy and dignity. We knew full well there was nothing the mayor was going to say that would turn the men around.

Loeb took his typical paternalistic line, saying he didn't understand what was wrong with the men, he was willing to give them the shirt off his back and he had known them and their fathers before them. It was an absolutely ridiculous performance. When I spoke, I addressed what I considered the

190

*issue to be: the question of the right of the workers to partici-
pate in those decisions that affect them. And I went through
what a contract ought to be from recognition to grievance.
Then the mayor came back and said he wasn't for any of that.
He was infuriated because he knew from the way the men sat
there, very stony and cold, that he had lost. He knew then he
had something very different on his hands. It also became very
clear to the men that the union was very important to them if
they were ever going to get the thing resolved.*

*On Thursday night the staff guys and local officers sat
down to make advance plans. We decided to hold meetings at
noon five days a week, take Saturday off and use Sunday as an
opportunity for the men to go to their churches and ask for
time to explain the situation to the congregation. We also
were beginning to worry about money. The strike was costing
quite a bit, and there was no pay for the workers, no strike
fund at all. We were reluctant even to talk about such a fund
because, as you can imagine, just ten bucks a head could run
up quite a tab. We were hoping some donations would come
from the churches.*

*We got some leaflets printed up, one to be distributed
downtown and another for the men to distribute along their
garbage routes. They were to explain our position, because in
a sanitation strike, particularly in a city like Memphis,
nobody understands or wants to understand. The papers
weren't helping us one damn bit.*

*As a result of our activity in the churches that first
Sunday a number of ministers came to our Monday meeting
along with some NAACP people and leaders of other labor
unions. The meetings were beginning to assume a religious
tone, for what was beginning to happen was a melding of religious feeling and our trade union attitudes about equality and
dignity.*

*Early in that second week we went back to see the mayor,
and by this time he was taking the position that we were
breaking the law and he wasn't even going to discuss it until*

191

the men went back to work. You have to visualize the scene in his office. He was sitting behind this monstrous desk which stands on a platform at least a foot above the floor. And behind him, mounted on the wall, is a model of a naval ship—I believe a PT boat—and it was a very contrived scene. There was a television camera pointing at Loeb, and every now and then the lights would go on, and he would go into a big tirade which would stop when the lights went out.

It was obvious the mayor was carrying on for the benefit of his redneck constituency, so Ciampa and I, being old demagogues ourselves, weren't going to be outdone. That was when Ciampa called him a liar and a dictator and told him to shut his big, fat mouth. That was filmed in living color, and when it came out that night we knew we were in this thing to the end. Ciampa's stock rose 200 percent in the black community because they had no idea anybody would talk to the mayor like that. The mayor's people even had bumper stickers printed with the words, CIAMPA GO HOME.

We never once picketed the work site. There was no need to, even though the mayor threatened to replace the striking workers, and maybe in a few cases he did. Then there was an interesting meeting in which the mayor agreed to appoint a committee of his people and we would appoint a committee of our people to see if together we couldn't boil some of the fat out of the thing. Joe Paisley and I represented our side, and we met in an anteroom of the mayor's office. Maybe one of the big tragedies of the whole thing is that during the course of that evening we reached agreement on all of the issues there were at that stage of the strike. The question of recognition, the question of grievances, the question of checkoff of union dues, although checkoff had not been an issue up to that point, they all seemed to be resolved. Then that same night we took the agreement to the mayor, and he just literally went ape. He said he couldn't agree to it, and he blew the meeting. But he agreed to meet again the next day.

The next day he was as reasonable as can be. He was a

192

different guy than he had been the night before. He explained to us his problems and said that surely we can find a way to resolve the thing. We allowed as how we hoped so, and we talked a little while, accomplished nothing further and adjourned. Then he went into a little back room, and by God if he didn't have a TV camera in there, and it filmed him as he yelled and screamed that he's not about to check off dues so the union can haul the money back to Washington, D.C. We didn't know that was going on until we caught the news that evening. What he did was set us up, and he scored a point by forcing the issue of checkoff. We tried to explain to the community that checkoff was no revolutionary idea, that United Fund contributions are checked off as are payments to loan companies.

We weren't getting anywhere with the mayor, so we decided to try the City Council. The chairman of the public works committee was a black councilman named Fred Davis, who knew as much about our situation as I knew about a flight to the moon. But we got him to call a meeting, and we tried to point out to the committee what the difficulty was and how simply it could be resolved. Davis pulled that old politician's line of how we didn't represent anyone so he didn't have to talk with us. We sent word back to the rubber workers hall where the men were standing by that it was time to show Davis we did represent somebody, and pretty soon the City Council chambers were filled to the brim with sanitation workers. Davis began screaming, "You can't address this committee like this, you can't coerce us, you can't intimidate us," but all the men were doing was sitting there very patiently waiting for the committee to take some action. It was our first sit-in demonstration. They just sat there, and we just sat there.

That city building was brand spanking new, and with its flaming red carpet and mahogany desks it was beautiful, so what we did next really appalled the committee. It was lunch time, so we sent out for bologna, salami, mayonnaise, mustard and bread, spread it all out on the council table and

193

started making sandwiches. The police began crowding into the place, but they didn't know what to do because all we were doing was eating. The only way they could eject us would have been to tear gas the place, and they weren't about to do that to that new building. Finally the committee passed a resolution we could live with and promised to put it before the full council the next morning. It was after five in the afternoon when we left, and I must say the council chamber was as clean as it had been before we arrived.

In the third week of the strike we formed the skeleton of what was to be COME, or Committee on the March for Equality. The significance of this was that in a basically anti-union city, the strike and our union were the central core of a unified, community effort to stand up to the establishment.

The City Council was leery of letting us back into its chambers, so its meeting was held in Ellis Auditorium. It was an incredible kind of session, like an old town meeting, but the strike was discussed in only a peripheral way. Then the council adjourned, and the crowd—not just workers but ministers and other community leaders—was really angry. They wanted to address the council, not rabblerouse, and the council simply marched out.

There was pandemonium for a moment as we decided what to do next. People were genuinely angry. We went outside, and Wurf was asking where we could meet. The rubber workers hall was too far away, so we decided on the Mason Temple which is a church of the United Church of Christ. There were police all over the place, and given the mood of our people, it was not the right time for them to be there. Jerry decided something had to be done to let off steam and to reach some understanding with the cops. He found the officer in charge, a captain, and got him to agree we could march to the Mason Temple. It was understood we could walk on the west side of Main Street and that cops would be posted along the way so the marchers would be protected, from what I never knew.

We started marching four abreast, but those cops had

194

their cars positioned in a way that we were forced closer and closer to the curb. At first we didn't think it was deliberate, but pretty soon we realized something was wrong, and the march just stopped all of a sudden right in the center of town. Then the cops proceeded to whip out their riot gear and spray the crowd with mace and beat us with their clubs. The cops didn't know a marcher from an onlooker, and they beat one as well as the other.

The members of the black establishment couldn't conceive of themselves being treated just like the strikers, but they were because it had become a black-white conflict. The city had decided that anyone who was black was anti, be he a banker, lawyer, minister or garbage man. If you were out there, it was just too bad. That brutal police action solidified what up to then had been pretty shaky support by the black community.

We spent the afternoon getting people out of jail and finding out who was in the hospital. That night we had a mass meeting at Mason Temple to make our battle plans. The COME crusade had now solidified, and we started getting endorsements we had not even expected before. It was a "dig in" thing.

The newspapers were not coming anywhere close to what actually was taking place. Our side wasn't getting told at all. We decided to boycott the papers since they were doing nothing for us anyway. We discussed the start of downtown marches to try to put pressure on the Chamber of Commerce, and we made plans to boycott the city merchants. By this time we were holding our noon meeting every day, as well as a church rally every night, and we were organized as committees to handle the various responsibilities. There was even a committee to arrange the meetings.

We began raising money in earnest, and we formed a strike support committee. We discovered some eye-opening facts. Here were men making $1.69 an hour and owing out more than they were taking in. The loan companies had such a hook into those guys that they were absolutely sold out for

195

the next 20 years. Refrigerators, television sets, cars—they were owing more on them after a couple of years than they did when they were new. I remember one guy who owed $1,350 on a 1958 Buick. We had made a commitment from a moral point of view that nobody would lose any material goods as a result of the strike, so we were paying for refrigerators that had been out of style for ten years. We'd help them out with money from contributions, and we would negotiate with the lenders, telling them, in some cases, we would continue interest payments but would not pay the principal.

The decisions of the strike support committee fell on yours truly, since the chairman of the Strike Support Committee was a local politician who didn't want to make anybody mad. It was hard. You can imagine if you have 1,300 guys on strike, 500 of them waiting in the hall for benefits, the situation can get chaotic.

By the fourth week the civil rights aspect of the action was quite evident, and one of the remarkable things is how we were able to keep a clear fix on our objective. It never totally became a civil rights fight or a religious crusade. It was always a trade union fight.

We had appealed to the community to try to be a leavening force and had managed to put together an interreligious group to serve as mediators, but as mediators typically do, they turned to the guy who was getting his brains beat out and gave the advice that we quit. I remember thinking how by extending that kind of logic they would probably let the city commit murder. There were five or six very prominent churchmen among the mediators and the best they could recommend is that the thing ought to be settled. They were sent packing.

Of course, the garbage was beginning to pile up, and that's a major inconvenience, but the community, the black community, did an amazing thing: they refused to let their trash be picked up. In at least one case I know about, scab sanitation workers were chased away by residents. The garbage was an effective weapon for us.

The ministers were trying desperately to put something together, and they prevailed on the mayor to sit down and discuss the issues again. Loeb had been out of it for a long time. The meeting was held one night in a church basement. He took his old stand: he didn't recognize the union and wouldn't speak directly to us. He addressed his remarks to an intermediary. Nothing came of that meeting.

We were aware after the strike had been going on for a month that we needed to apply some pressure by means of coverage by the press outside Memphis. We invited Bayard Rustin and Roy Wilkins, and they both showed up on the same day. We had hoped the national press would follow them, but it didn't. We got speeches and support, but that was it. Then we heard that Dr. King was coming through either Mississippi or Alabama, and Jim Lawson said he would try to schedule him in Memphis for just a speech. I'm not sure whether he said so immediately, but he did agree to come, and we began to mobilize for a big meeting at Mason Temple. The night he came there must have been 17,000 to 20,000 people there, and Dr. King delivered a tremendous speech and called for a march the following Friday. On that day Memphis was hit by its worst snowstorm in 30 years, and the march was postponed until the following Thursday.

On the day of the march I must say we did not read a number of things accurately. We did not understand the depth of hostility in the kids which was directed at the city but was caused partly by their inability to be involved in the action. And as the march got underway we realized there were no firm controls to prevent violence. When we heard windows being broken ahead of us, we knew that people in the march weren't doing it, and our first reaction was to make sure that the marchers didn't get caught up in it. We even were dragging people off the sidewalk into the march so we could keep control of them.

I think the cops were just as afraid as we were. Neither they nor we knew what to do. We were just a couple of blocks up Main Street when Lawson got a microphone and called the march to a halt, but by this time the cops had decided they had to make a move because they couldn't tolerate the window breaking. So they broke out the nightsticks and mace again, and it was just like the first time—indiscriminate beating and maceing of innocent people.

The march ended in chaos, and we were lucky no one else got hurt. We scheduled a meeting with Dr. King that night to discuss plans for the future.

Following our aborted march the National Guard came to Memphis, more for show than for a serious purpose. We were trying to figure out our next move, and it was clear that Dr. King was concerned about the impact of the violence. He was being blamed for it, and that did him very little good. He was returning to Atlanta, and Jerry and I drove him to the airport. We were to get back in touch with him after we had made a better assessment of the situation and after we'd had a meeting to decide where to head. But it was definite there would be another march, if for no other reason than to show the city we had not been driven off. And we decided that in going back we would really have to make sure the men understood what was at stake.

A couple of very surprising things took place. At our next meeting we were kind of down and couldn't decide if we ought to keep up the boycott and the marches. We met in the rubber workers hall and our decision was made for us by a guy in the back of the room who got up to ask, "Ain't we gonna march today?" The march was a big success, for here were these tired-ass marchers armed with nothing but their picket signs, passing by an arsenal of modern military weapons—jeeps, half tracks, machine guns and soldiers with fixed bayonets. It just happened that some of the national newsmen had stayed around, so we got our national press coverage.

Dr. King cancelled a trip to Africa and returned to Memphis to lead another march. The night he arrived he made his famous "I've been to the mountain" speech. That was Wednesday. The march was planned for Friday, but on Thursday evening King was killed.

198

Everybody and his brother was trying by this time to get meetings scheduled between the city and us. A committee of businessmen was set up to help settle the dispute. We weren't having any luck at all with the mayor, and the City Council had washed its hands of the problem. I think the assassination was a catalyst in arranging renewed negotiations, although it didn't have much effect on an eventual settlement. The city was most concerned about the fact it might have tarnished its image; it wasn't that it was too bad King was killed, but that he had been killed in Memphis. The Chamber of Commerce was very upset, and it was businessmen's pressure that forced the mayor into meeting with us.

Jim Reynolds, the undersecretary of labor, came to Memphis, and I think we would still be negotiating had it not been for him. It was his kind of skill that got the thing worked out. Jerry and Ciampa and I still were very much involved. We had to be, for we had got the community so deeply involved we could not afford to do anything that would appear to be giving up the struggle.

We were making progress. We were able to overcome the grievance procedure thing, we were able to overcome the recognition problem, although the mayor was still playing games with checkoff. Jerry suggested, as he has in other negotiations, that the city needn't get involved with checkoff; it could turn it over to the credit union. The mayor regarded that as some sort of subterfuge, but then we learned the credit union was an independent, employee-run system over which the mayor had no control. Our members could have their dues deducted, and there was nothing the mayor could do about it.

It was a good settlement. We made the promotional system stand up, and they now have a sound setup based on seniority and competence. We completely changed the nature of the work; for one thing it's no longer all black here and all white there. The grievance procedure has probably been adjusted since I was there, but it works, and they guard it with shotguns.

As we were going over the final agreement there was one

199

last stumbling block: T.O. Jones decided not to sign. He wasn't bothered by any particular point; he simply wanted to reescalate the demands. We retired to a private room, and while I advised him how nice life would be for him on another planet, Ciampa suggested to him numerous forms of torture he would never forget. Jones decided to sign.

After we got about all we thought we could, we decided to test the contract on the community group because it had been an important factor all through the strike. So there were two meetings to approve the agreement, one with community leaders at the Sheraton-Peabody Hotel and the final one with the men at Clayborn Temple. We presented it to them provision by provision, and the ratification was a delightful sight to behold.

The strike lasted 65 days, and it took another week to wrap things up, so I was away quite a bit longer than I had expected. I believe my parking bill at the airport in Detroit was the largest in the history of the union. It was $148.50.

Wurf: Thoughts About Equality

I am from a minority ethnic group, brought up understanding that some people have access to the benefits of society, other people have limited access, others have no access. In my day access to graduate school was denied not only to blacks but to Jews and even some Catholics. I come out of a milieu that is opposed to manipulation of trade unions by Communists, but also opposed to the mentality that is common in some trade union circles—to brand as Communists anyone or anything that takes a strong or radical position.

There were important changes taking place. For instance, when I first worked with the Congress on Racial Equality or CORE, it was an integrated organization, and whites had as much input as blacks because whites had more access to money and institutions. I admit that when Stokely Carmichael began screaming about black power and arguing

200

that whites should be excluded from the struggle, I felt offended. I thought to myself, I'm an old freedom marcher, and these guys are busting me out.

Well, I was both right and wrong. Right because racism—black, brown, white or pink—is still racism. But for the same reason I believe in a collective bargaining relationship, equity at the bargaining table as opposed to being a supplicant, I can understand why blacks need to feel they can find solutions to their problems without the help of whites. There's a certain patronizing that goes with that help that is less than comfortable to men who are concerned with dignity.

I like to tell our training institutes what most organizers don't realize. They think they're peddling better wages and working conditions, but essentially they're offering dignity. And sometimes the worker who doesn't articulate this very easily has more awareness than the professional organizer.

The civil rights struggle, the equality struggle or whatever you want to call it, is just one part of this continuing struggle for dignity.

That's the starting point. One might say you then move with caution with a prearranged plan, but that's a crock. You decide that you'll take the bitter with the better. You have no idea how traumatic it is to find some SOB who is black running for office just because he's black. And then you find his goddamn white opponent is doing exactly the same thing. It isn't the better of the two men; it's the whitest and blackest of the two men that is going to decide the election.

There's a quick growing up process about things. The simple becomes more complicated, like the Memphis strike. That routine sanitation workers' strike became one of the most significant experiences of my life.

It was soon clear it was difficult, it was a mess, and I went down there and ran into something I had read about but never really understood or encountered. The white power structure of a southern city is quite different face to face than from a distance.

There was also the problem of getting accepted by the

201

black power structure, which is split into 98 fragments and basically anti-union. I understood quickly the influence of the black church. Its impact on the black community was something I'd known about theoretically but never really understood.

I soon realized this strike was not just an economic struggle against an employer. It was for real, a struggle against a mayor who had made racism the keystone of his election platform. He had been in office only 40 days when the strike began, and his campaign slogan had been something like, "Let's bring Dixie back to Memphis." It was a traumatic experience to discover this mayor was a Jew, that Jews can be guilty of bigotry and Jews can be identified with the overdog as well as the underdog. There is a Jewish power structure in Memphis. The Jewish leaders may have felt sympathetic, but they didn't want some trade union guy digging up shit in the community where they had been accepted. Maybe they still couldn't join the Memphis Country Club, but short of that they were in. Remember, this is the city that produced Abe Fortas, the former Supreme Court justice.

I became intimate with the black community at three levels. I got to know the successful black businessman. I got to know the black bourgeois, ministers and teachers generally, a tough, pragmatic group of men who had escaped the cotton fields the way my forefathers escaped from Polish ghettos. And I got to know the black workers, tragic men who had started out chopping cotton for two or three bucks a day, finally made it from Mississippi to Memphis and got a job with the sanitation department for six or seven bucks a day. They were treated with contempt, having to tip their hats to their white bosses until they revolted.

We understood we couldn't win in the usual way, because this wasn't a usual labor-management scrap. It was a freedom struggle, and we had to call on the national black leadership for help.

King was reluctant to come. He had made several futile efforts to get a movement going in Memphis, with no success.

202

Besides, this was a time when King, a Nobel Peace Prize winner and a substantial figure, had fallen on his face in Chicago. He was trying to resurrect his image with the poverty demonstrations, the Poor People's March on Washington.

We were able to persuade King to come through an influential Memphis preacher, Jim Lawson, who was close to King. What a meeting we had! Every black in the community— 15,000 to 16,000 of them—filled the hall. I spoke and everybody connected with the strike spoke in a black church every night thereafter.

I wasn't in Memphis the day King was killed. I had come back to Washington to talk to Meany about help. Let it be said about Meany: he wanted to help settle the strike. On April 4 Ames and I met with Meany and Lane Kirkland, the AFL-CIO secretary-treasurer, and Meany agreed to set up a national fund raising committee which he would kick off with a contribution of $20,000 from the AFL-CIO. He would also contact every affiliate of the federation to get their support, and he promised a press statement the following day to announce his intentions.

When I got home I took Mildred and our son, Nicholas, shopping, and there was a message to call Ames when we got back. Joe told me King had been shot, and while we talked he heard a TV bulletin that it was fatal.

I remember trying to get down to Memphis to put something together. Guys kept coming to the house, union staffers mostly and Eric Polisar who went with me. My first thought was we just had to put an end to the strike. Throughout the strike, as we did later to other strikes of this kind—in Huntsville and Atlanta—we kept the city non-violent. Now I was afraid that the holy indignity that had been heaped on these people would cause the whole community to blow.

Memphis didn't burn, but King was dead, and after it was over I felt that if these people could only be liberated—I mean blacks all over America—it would turn loose an important force for a better country.

203

Poised bayonets along demonstration route (above) tell the tenseness of the Memphis confrontation; faces of striking workers (below) explain how it all began

10. Power as a 'Countervailing Force for Good'

At every level of our union, there has been a tremendous activity and progress. And perhaps the most active single person in the Union has been our International President, Jerry Wurf.

Not too many of you who are here today were with us in Denver eight years ago when our Union of 230,000 members changed administrations and changed direction. Those who were there will agree with me, I think, that those were rather dark days in this Union, with division, suspicion, lethargy, and conflict holding us back.

President Wurf came to that convention as the Executive Director of District Council 37 in New York. That Council had grown from just a handful of members in 1948, when he became an organizer among New York City employees, to a major power within the Union with some 40,000 members.

That convention in Denver was a benchmark for this union. We moved quickly into a constitutional convention in 1965 and into the greatest period of growth of the decade for an American union.

Today, we are the sixth largest union in the AFL-CIO, the fastest-growing union in the country, and the largest public employee union in the Western Hemisphere. I say to you that none of this is due

entirely to the leadership of our International Presi-
dent, but that all of it reflects the quality and vigor
of his service to the Union.

Joseph Ames
19th International Convention of AFSCME
May 29, 1972

Wurf's office in Washington reflects his personality and his background. It is a large, handsome office, functional yet warm and comfortable. In contrast to the tastefully decorated modern furnishings, an old pawnbroker's clock hangs near his desk, the lettering on the glass covering the pendulum reads: "H. Cohen, Jeweler, 502 Broad Street, Terms if Desired." The walls are filled with pictures, line drawings and items of interest to Wurf, although notably missing are those stock shots—sometimes called Washington wallpaper—of Wurf shaking hands with dignitaries. One wall holds a photograph of the Boston police strike in 1919, and a picture of the first AFSCME convention in 1936.

On another wall is a framed enlargement of an old union record. Dated March 10, 1948, it is a copy of the paysheet for Wurf's first six months with the union, his trial period. Two facts are noted at the bottom: he had been rehired, and he had convinced the administration that in addition to his salary, which remained at $60 a week, he would be given $60 a month expenses.

As Joe Ames noted at the 1972 convention, much had changed since Wurf joined AFSCME on March 10, 1948.

Col. A.E. Garey had died. Arnold Zander was in semi-retirement in Green Bay, Wisconsin, spending his time teaching at the University of Wisconsin branch there or taking part in activities of several international organizations. Leo Kramer was president of his own company, Leo Kramer, Inc., a general research firm that does business in Washington. Gordon Chapman, Bill McEntee and most of the old-time international executive board members were in retirement.

206

Of the original band who helped Wurf to victory in 1964, the "not-so-young turks," most were still active in the union. Ames, who had served from 1966 to 1972 as secretary-treasurer of the international union, had become chairman of the Judicial Panel, the body that arbitrates internal disputes and election disagreements. Al Bilik was assistant to the president for organization, Father Blatz was an international vice-president. Vic Gotbaum was still executive director of District Council 37, and Tom Morgan and Norm Schut were officials of their home base organizations in Ohio and the state of Washington respectively.

Only Hastings was no longer with the union. After five years as Wurf's top aide he had moved to direct the Labor Relations Training Center of the U.S. Civil Service Commission.

The revolution was over, the reforms had been instituted and the work continued. As Wurf told the delegates in 1972:

> We enter our 19th International Convention as a union still engaged in the effort of changing from collective begging to collective bargaining. The effort continues, but the name of the game has changed. We are established and stable. We have matured and reached the point where we stand in the front ranks of the labor movement. Our growth and size make us strong, and the services we are able to provide our membership makes us effective and influential. . . .

In 1972 AFSCME membership was over 500,000, including public employees in 47 states, the District of Columbia and two territories (Panama Canal Zone and Puerto Rico). Only Alaska, South Carolina and Idaho were not represented. The members were divided into 2,400 locals and approximately 70 councils, with 24,000 elected officers. By this time at least two-thirds of the members were blue-collar workers, and there were nearly 100,000 members working in hospitals and nursing homes.

207

According to Charles Culhane of *The National Journal*, which did a major study of AFSCME in late 1971:

> While the members are scattered around the country, about 80 percent of the membership is concentrated in about 13 states, the District of Columbia and the Panama Canal Zone. The union's stronghold is New York City where some 92,000 members work for the city government. . . .
>
> The councils and the local unions exercise a high degree of autonomy in collective bargaining with state and local governments. The national staff generally involves itself in bargaining only at the request of local leaders.

What had happened was that the power base of the union had turned around. The small locals had been Arnold Zander's strength, and he was thus able to dominate the union under the old voting rules. Once that voting system had been eliminated, the organization changed to reflect more accurately where the power lay in terms of numbers of members. Giving the big locals and councils their share of the power not only signaled Zander's defeat, but it led to a new era of growth for the union.

Wurf spoke on another point in his opening address to the 1972 convention, a point that was getting a lot of attention in the general press. It was the old question of the right to strike but he gave it a new twist.

> The biggest barrier to achieving reasonable mechanisms is the question of impasse procedures, i.e. when the boss is willing to be reasonable. Labor has traditionally opposed compulsory arbitration. I have news for you. The bosses we work for are scared to death of it. The employers who deny us the right to strike fear compulsory arbitration even more. They have seen third party neutrals grant

some extremely fair and reasonable settlements. Because of this fear of arbitration, the bosses may be coming around on the right to strike. Some of them are, most want to deny us any form of final step in impasse procedure that takes any measure of control out of their hands. They want to leave us under their thumb. They want control, not reasonableness. They cannot have it their way on this one. It is time to reason together. We are prepared to do that. We are willing to experiment, to consider new means of impasse procedures. However, our expressions of willingness to try voluntary binding arbitration—jointly agreed to by labor and management—thus far have fallen on uninterested ears.

In the tradition of labor's most progressive leaders Wurf was taking the play away from the immediate issue—the right to strike—by suggesting a new and better idea as far as public employee unionism was concerned. In an interview with journalist William J. Eaton, who was doing a report on public employee unions for the Labor-Management Relations Service (of the National League of Cities-U.S. Conference of Mayors-National Association of Counties), Wurf elaborated on the same point.

WURF: Nobody ever prints this but I say it to our staff and I say it to our membership. I am opposed to strikes. I don't want strikes. They're bad. They're hard on the city but they're harder on the workers. I fight bitterly for the right to strike—the *right* to strike. But I don't think there's any principle involved in striking. Striking is a tactic to persuade an employer to deal with us. If it can be avoided, almost any price ought to be paid in order to avoid a strike.

Q. You seem to be cozying up to some kind of arbitration procedure?

209

WURF: That's a very perceptive statement. I've been saying to management: "Why don't you try us out on arbitration?" but there have been no takers.

Q. Can you expand a little on that?

WURF: Like any traditional trade unionist, I'm a little scared of arbitration . . . my fear is that an arbitrator likes to go down the middle . . . takes a survey of 10 similar groups, splits the difference and tries to maintain parity. I think the role of a trade union . . . is to plow new frontiers. I want to get new and better things but the arbitrator may not be willing to give them. But the thing that's impressed me is that some arbitrators understand that (viewpoint) and some don't . . . I don't want statutory, compulsive arbitration. But I would be quite willing to enter into an agreement with an employer that after 60 days or 30 days of negotiation, if we can't reach a settlement, that we submit the matter to arbitration or the unresolved matters to arbitration. In other words, exhaust the collective bargaining process and then go to arbitration and try to win the case . . . Without committing myself to statutory, mandatory arbitration, I am saying that I am ready and willing to recommend to our locals and councils that they test some mechanism for arbitrating disputes.

Wurf's position on arbitration was not something brand new. He had been moving in that direction for years. In a speech to AFSCME Council 17 in Baton Rouge, Louisiana on March 23, 1969 he gave his general position, "The way you stop strikes in the public service is by giving justice to the workers, not by frightening them or coercing them or threatening them." He went on to explain his attitude toward strikes. First, he reviewed the recent anti-strike legislation in

210

numerous states, carefully spelling out the details of the laws and in particular the penalties for violations.

Well, let me say why I've been giving you all of this information. I'm leading up to something, and this is the first time I've talked about it publicly. In essence, we have been trying to do something in all of the states to develop a machinery of reasonableness and fair play for public employees. And we just don't get it. We find ourselves in the incredibly ridiculous position of making speeches about strikes, and we don't want to strike. We just want some machinery for doing our job.

Later that same year, in July, he would expound on the theme of AFSCME's attitude toward strikes while a radio guest on WINS in New York City. After mentioning that he had seen, "back on page 63 of the newspaper," that doctors and druggists were threatening to strike because they might lose money dealing with Medicare patients, Wurf discussed the growing talk of strikes.

Everybody is striking against everybody, but somehow everyone gets very sanctimonious when it comes to public employees. Well I would agree that certain vital services can't stop. I, for example, would suggest that nobody got over-excited in this town when Con Edison went out on strike, and that was a much more devastating strike than any public employee strike you ever had with the possible exception of the subway strike. And, there's been a storm . . .

Q. Are you equating a Con Ed strike with, say, a strike by police and firemen?

WURF: . . . Well let me very carefully say that I don't believe police and firemen have a right to strike, and our union constitution says so, and I've made that point time and time again. But I am saying to you that a strike of Con Ed is a very serious matter, and I think the union very reluctantly and very seldom goes out on strike. And some years ago there were some laws to prevent these strikes, but you know, the bosses moved to get rid of the laws, because all the laws did was act as a provocation to bring on more utility strikes. If you had grey hair, you'd remember . . . But let me say this, nobody wants to go out on strike. Nobody wants to leave the bedside of a patient, nobody want to leave garbage uncollected, nobody wants to leave a hole in a highway, nobody wants to leave a typewriter in city hall. People go out on strike—and, you know, public employees are essentially conservative people—out of sheer desperation. And I tell you that public officials by their irresponsibility bring this out.

In the interview for *The National Journal* Wurf made the additional point that he would fight for a federal law that would make collective bargaining a national right. "What we run into is not hostility (to a federal law requiring collective bargaining by state and local governments) except in the most reactionary circles. What Congressmen are concerned about is what this will mean to their relationships with mayors, county officials and state officials. I think the day is coming when the law will be passed."

Wurf concluded his remarks to the 1972 convention by explaining his aspirations for AFSCME and the American labor movement. His vision represents the logical fulfillment of a quarter of a century of effort and experience.

If we can get rid of the wars of jurisdictional warfare, we can get on with the important business of organizing the unorganized. We can build strength rather than dissipate power. A stronger labor movement will be more representative, more credible. With that power of organization the American labor movement can be more what it should be, which is a countervailing force for good. Our society is threatened by the absence of such a force. Labor needs economic, political, and social clout. Strong labor union organization provides a climate of economic reasonableness and political responsiveness.

The first and plainest responsibility of this union is to deal with the parochial social and economic needs of public employees. We're going to keep those concerns as our first priority. But as we gain in size and strength and prestige, we also gain new responsibilities—especially our responsibility to work for a better trade union movement and a better America.

Samuel Gompers, the founder of the American Federation of Labor, was once asked what labor wanted. His reply was "more." My definition of "more"—and the definition that I think this union lives by—is that this labor movement can be a force for not just the economic well-being of workers, but for peace, tranquility, and a better tomorrow for all mankind.

In the 1970's there was no doubt among labor observers that Wurf had accomplished his internal reform program and thereby kept his campaign promises. Haynes Johnson and Nick Kotz of *The Washington Post,* in their 1972 series on the American labor movement, gave AFSCME the highest marks. They pointed out that the union was the only one to grow substantially at a time when the rest of the movement seemed to be faltering:

. . . The early labor movement, as the present

213

one, was marred by imperfections, by excesses and by positions over which honest men can disagree in a democracy. The American Federation of Labor of the 1890's had narrow and selfish interests, as do most American institutions. But it also had idealism.

"We want more schoolhouses and less jails, more books and less arsenals, more learning and less vice, more constant work and less crime, more leisure less greed, more justice and less revenge," said Samuel Gompers, the first AFL president, nearly 80 years ago.

His kind of vision lives on in the labor movement today. Jerry Wurf, president of the American Federation of State, County and Municipal Employees, spelled out the imperfections and promises of organized labor.

As we have already said, Wurf's union is a model of vitality and democracy. Membership in Wurf's union is voluntary; you do not have to pay dues or receive the union's permission to work. It is also a union that works incessantly at communicating with its members and in espousing causes that many other unions shun. . . .

. . . Wurf said:

"The litmus test of a free society is a vital labor movement. Sorry as our labor movement has been at times in its history, I think you'll find that the vigor of a society is closely related to the vigor of the trade union movement.

"And I would say to you that if you have a dull, meaningless, unconcerned labor movement, you'll find there's a very important lack in the society in its narrowest and broadest sense."

Other journals from *Reader's Digest* to *The Nation* have

observed AFSCME's rise, and all agree the union could become the largest single union in the AFL-CIO. As to the potential effect of AFSCME and other public employee unions, William L. Abbott wrote in *The Nation,* "Public worker unions enjoy a soaring increase in members. This reshuffling of power will renovate the House of Labor. It will never be the same again."

In his column in *Newsday* Patrick Owens gave the union and Wurf in particular very high praise in July 1972, calling Wurf a new Reuther, a ". . . 53-year-old wunderkind of the geriatric AFL-CIO."

> AFSCME is in a position to grow. It is the biggest and busiest union of public employees and they are almost the only workers who are joining unions these days. But Wurf has moved with extraordinary energy and considerable shrewdness to maintain the growth rate and to harness AFSCME's burgeoning resources. A tireless traveler and, like Reuther, a blue-streak talker, Wurf is a wonder to behold as he tours a strike front, his gawky body hustling down a picket line or his compelling, rather rough voice exhorting a picket line.

> Like Reuther, Wurf is a social activist and an intellectual. A major difference is that he is also a great "so-what?" man. He enjoys theoretical speculation, but likes to cut through it to the immediate point.

It is not only the growth and potential of the union that has attracted the media to Jerry Wurf. A large factor has been that in the '70s Wurf is one of the few voices within the inner council of the AFL-CIO (of which he is a vice-president) that dares to oppose George Meany. As *Time* said in 1973, "at meetings of the AFL-CIO executive council, says one insider, the vote usually ranges from 25-to-1 to 34-to-1, depending on how many other union chiefs are present to vote down Jerry Wurf."

Wurf's opposition to Meany, for whom he has enormous respect, is complex. An ideological ally of Reuther, Wurf nevertheless stood by the AFL-CIO president in the feud that led ultimately to Reuther's withdrawal of the United Auto Workers from the federation in 1968. Wurf did so because he believes, despite their differences, that Meany's philosophy—tough and pragmatic, even though not so concerned about social values—is in the best interest of the labor movement.

The differences are by no means unimportant. They disagreed over U.S. involvement in the Vietnam war (AFSCME voted resolutions against it at three consecutive conventions) and over the McGovern candidacy for president in 1972. They concur in their opposition to Nixon, although their reasons are not entirely similar. "A substantial reason old anti-Communist Meany hates Nixon is the détente with Russia," Wurf has said somewhat disapprovingly. "And Meany feels betrayed by Nixon on the Watergate scandal." They also have fundamental differences over what Wurf feels is an urgent need to organize the unorganized.

There is another reason why the general press and labor periodicals pay frequent attention to Wurf and his union. In 1971 Wurf took steps to make his idea of increased political strength for public employees a reality. In alliance with the International Association of Fire Fighters and the huge National Education Association he formed the Coalition of American Public Employees (CAPE) to lobby in Washington on behalf of a potential membership of 3,000,000 workers. The goals of the organization, which is not a union but a political action alliance, are to push for a federal collective bargaining law for state and local government employees, repeal of the Hatch Act (which forbids government employees to engage in partisan political activity) and a broad range of legislative measures of interest to members of the alliance. One recent success was the inclusion of government employees, at all levels, in the provisions of a federal bill providing for minimum wage and overtime benefits.

216

In an article on CAPE in January 1973 *Newsweek* evaluated its potential for success. "For one thing, it will be headed by the dynamic Wurf, who is widely regarded as one of the most savvy operators on the labor scene today. For another, the opportunity for growth is enormous."

Thus in less than a decade Wurf has become a labor leader with real power, his union is financially and internally healthy, infused with a philosophy of progress and social awareness. Even though it continues to grow at a rate of 1,000 members per week, AFSCME is just beginning to tap the potential of public employees whose numbers are now estimated to be approximately 13.5 million, with more growth to come.

The 1964 revolution within AFSCME had many parallels in society at large. America was still mourning President Kennedy as it geared up for the Great Society and began an unprecedented effort to alleviate social problems. Most of the major figures of those years did not survive the decade, and few of the ambitious plans, much less the dreams, became realities. Yet AFSCME grew in strength and power by applying not just the principles of those years but also some of the newer goals, equality for women, for example.

The men and women who engineered the revolt that produced the AFSCME of today are still, for the most part, busily engaged in the continuing work of the union. What it was like to live through those early years of change was perhaps best expressed by Bob Hastings: "Those were thrilling times. Damn, when you get right down to it, I really miss that union."

Wurf: Dynamic of Dignity

Things are beginning to happen, attention is being paid to us. I'm being invited to speak at forums on subjects of substance. What is happening is our union is becoming the spokesman, the pattern-setter, the theoretician for our public employee organization. People are really beginning to notice our existence.

217

Key labor guys are beginning to call me to get my point of view, and whether they agree or not, relationships are developing. We're beginning to take on status, credibility, meaningfulness. Obviously there are doubts and reservations in some areas of the labor movement, not about anything in particular, but because as Meany would say, I'm just not as "predictable" as they like the boys to be. But we can't be overlooked, and that is why I ended up on the AFL-CIO executive council.

The route to go is an honest, defensible position, and push it. Support a candidate who is worthy of support. If you have a decent position and push it, you don't have to go to the boss as a beggar, you go to him as an equal. You demand participation in the mechanism that is going to decide your destiny. Even when you lose—in New York we didn't support a winner for a generation until John Lindsay got elected—it's important to stand and be counted.

The most important dynamic in our organization is the conferring of dignity on workers, whether they're engineers or trash collectors, whether they're conservative or radical, and that's what I mean when I talk about the dynamic of dignity. The be all and end all is dignity.

Something is happening in America that is critical, and that is the work force has crossed the line, the majority is no longer working in manufacturing but in service. Now the importance of that is this: historically the part that is organized, better paid, able to influence legislation is the industrial work force, as opposed to the service work force. But now this change is occurring, and the place where it's showing up in very big numbers is in local and state government.

Outgoing Secretary-Treasurer Joe Ames (left) and Jerry Wurf congratulating William Lucy on being elected to succeed Ames, at the union's 1972 convention in Houston

219

Seafarers President Hall congratulates Wurf at a dinner honoring the new AFSCME president in 1965

220

Reflections of a Philosophic Sailor

Wurf has been knocked down so many times he must have callouses on his ass. In our language, he started in the hold, and it was a long struggle just to get on deck. I don't know of any labor leader in America who had a tougher fight—from shit to millions, from a little hall in Queens talking to two dozen people to a packed Madison Square Garden.

Paul Hall, president,
Seafarers International Union
January 10, 1974

Despite the biased atmosphere, the perfect vantage point from which to view the AFSCME record and Wurf's career is the third "deck" of the Seafarers International Union hall in Brooklyn. Paul Hall knows Wurf better than any other labor leader, and although his admiration is boundless, he can also see the warts.

"He's the greatest fighter I've ever worked with," says Hall, "a rugged guy who can hang in tough, even though he's often been the underdog. Wurf did more for public workers in a few years than the industrial unions accomplished in a century. But unlike the Queen of England, an activist attracts enemies, and there are those who feel he's done too much."

Wurf was still with the Hotel and Restaurant Employees when he and Hall first teamed up in 1947. White collar

221

employees of the New York Stock Exchange went on st
union security, the first such action of its kind, a very
and brutal strike, Hall remembers. Although the New
Central Body stood aside, AFL President William Green
the SIU to put its muscle on the line, because the white
workers "had never taken a walk before."

"I was later reminded of the Wall Street strike when
Russians took over Czechoslovakia," Hall relates. "The c
beat a lot of heads, but Wurf came through it like
champion."

Shortly thereafter Wurf became staff representative of
AFSCME in New York at a time when, as Hall puts it, "the
national union was as screwed up as a Chinese fire and boat
drill." And Wurf was *persona non grata* among the New York
labor hierarchy, as shown by the opposition he encountered
from the Teamsters, a nemesis to this day. The late Martin
Lacey, then president of both the Teamsters Joint Council and
the New York Central Body, succeeded in splintering Wurf's
organization by luring away John DeLury, then as now leader
of the sanitation workers, and the late Henry Feinstein.

"Wurf assumed leadership with nothing to lead," says
Hall, and Lacey was ruthless in the way he set out to do Wurf
in. Their basic differences were philosophical, because Wurf
has a strong social conscience, while Lacey represented the
trâditional labor concept of everything for the sake of a
contract."

A second source of friction was Lacey's relationship with
City Hall. Depending on which mayor, weak or strong,
occupied the office, Lacey either controlled or was controlled
by him. Either way, he resented the threat to this arrangement
by a union official who regarded the mayor as the boss, the
opposition across a bargaining table.

"Wurf was interfering with the system," says Hall, "so
the AFL was dedicated to the proposition that he would not get
off the ground and fly."

Wurf had but one friend in the organized labor

ent, and it was the SIU. Hall explained why:

First of all, we were impressed with the way he handled himself in the Wall Street strike, but it went much deeper than that. A sailor has damn few friends who aren't other sailors. But there was a time when we were underdogs too, so we decided to give him a hand. We helped him, but he helped us too, especially our younger seamen who have a lot to learn from a philosophical man. He wasn't like the damn Stalinists and Trotskyites who were never around when the asses were getting busted and the legs were getting popped.

Sailors generally distrust political people, but Wurf proved they all aren't phony. Many of our men, their memories fogged by the years, think Jerry is an old sailor too.

Having stayed with him through the tough period, Hall regards Wurf's more recent success as vindication of his loyalty. He regards his old buddy from Brooklyn, as "a restless warrior and a builder who leads an organization destined to be the biggest in the movement, a leader who has brought increased dignity to the public worker, no longer the object of contempt."

Hall admires the fact that Wurf has even been able to change the laws of certain states, and he is especially fond of some innovative techniques, like the time Wurf put elephants on the picket line during a zoo strike. Hall also is aware that an activist like Wurf will offend more complacent people and even ambitious ones who feel threatened.

Wurf's relationship with the rest of the movement could be much better, and now is the time he should develop it. The guys who have found Jerry troublesome would feel differently if they really got to know him. His problems are by no

223

means unusual. Labor has a history of fights—t
steel workers versus the sheet metal workers, f
example, or the auto workers versus the machinists

Hall cites two contributions as the greatest Wui
made, but he is uncertain which stands ahead of the c
One is the national recognition he has gained for the pe
he represents, "the injection of legitimate trade unionism
the public employee structure." In Hall's view pu
employees no longer are "half-assed hacks, captives of cl
house politicians." The other, in very simple terms, is t
Wurf has built a great union.

> Jerry never takes things lightly. His greatest asset
> is his loyalty to his members. He never sees a crowd,
> he sees people. He will go to the wall for the little
> guy whose ass is hanging down.
> The problem is that he fights the preliminary
> bouts as if they were the main event, always at full
> steam. He needs to learn to pace himself. If he con-
> serves his strength and parlays his opportunities,
> there is no limit to what he can do.
> In politics and international affairs he and I are
> way apart, but in what matters—the business of
> trade unionism—he is number one. Like the fighter
> who made it through all those dirty, little towns, he
> deserves to be in Madison Square Garden.

224